The Preacher's Paperback Library
Edmund A. Steimle, Consulting Editor

Renewal

in the

Pulpit

Sermons by

YOUNGER PREACHERS

Edited and with an Introduction by

EDMUND A. STEIMLE

FORTRESS PRESS • PHILADELPHIA

ABOUT THE

PREACHER'S PAPERBACK LIBRARY

The renewal of the church in our time has touched many aspects of parish life: liturgy and sacraments, biblical and theological concern, the place of the laity, work with small groups. But little has been said or done with regard to the renewal of the church in the pulpit.

The Preacher's Paperback Library is offered in the hope that it will contribute to the renewal of the preaching ministry. It will not stoop to providing "sermon starters" or other homiletical gimmicks. It will, rather, attempt to hold in balance the emphasis which contemporary theologians and biblical scholars lay upon the centrality of proclamation and the very practical concerns of theological students and parish pastors who are engaged in the demanding task of preparing sermons of biblical and theological depth which also speak to the contemporary world.

To that end, the series will provide reprints of fundamental homilectical studies not presently available and contemporary studies in areas of immediate concern to the preacher. Moreover, because the study of sermons themselves can be of invaluable help in every aspect of the preparation of the sermon, volumes of sermons with introductory notes will appear from time to time. The sermons will include reprints of outstanding preachers in the past as well as sermons by contemporary preachers who have given evidence both of depth and of imaginative gifts in communication. It is our hope that each volume in The Preacher's Paperback Library, prepared with the specific task of sermon preparation in mind, will contribute to the renewal of the preaching ministry.

EDMUND A. STEIMLE

Union Theological Seminary
New York, New York
Pentecost, 1966

CONTENTS

The Hard, Knotty Problems of the Faith

INTRODUCTION

This volume of sermons by younger Lutheran preachers had its origin in a hunch: that some of the best preaching in America today is being done by men no more than ten years out of seminary. To test the hunch, the field had to be restricted to make it manageable; hence the limitation with respect to Lutheran preachers.

Letters were sent to professors of homiletics in all Lutheran theological seminaries in North America requesting them to submit names of younger men who, in their judgment, showed unusual promise as preachers while in the seminary. A list of well over one hundred and fifty names was compiled from this major source as well as from others and again letters were sent out asking for sermon manuscripts. The response was so overwhelming that the project almost died of abundance. But out of the several hundred manuscripts submitted, these twenty-two were finally selected. They are offered here, however, not merely to justify a hunch.

These sermons are offered as evidence that renewal in the church is going on not only in the more familiar patterns of the ecumenical movement, lay activity, evangelism, biblical theology and stewardship. Martin Marty comments: "Few are ready to add 'renewal of preaching' to this list and then to document it." [1] We are bold enough to submit these twenty-two sermons as documentation for the "renewal of preaching" in our time. The fact that only

[1] Martin E. Marty. *Second Chance for American Protestants.* (New York: Harper & Row. 1963). p. 160.

twenty-two out of several hundred sermons are here offered might seem to undercut the value of the documentation were it not for the additional fact that a far larger number of the sermons submitted, though not perhaps appropriate for publication, showed many of the characteristics which appear so strongly in this collection.

What, then, are the issues involved in the current discussion of church renewal which these sermons reflect?

To begin with, you will find no appeals here for the support of the church as an institution. These preachers have moved well beyond the institution-centered sermon. The institution is assumed, not defended. Some parish ministers might react acidly, pointing to the fact that only one contributor is currently serving a parish church! No wonder they do not feel constrained to call for support of the institution. But this is not the complete picture. Six of these sermons were delivered when their authors were serving parish churches, and six more were delivered in the context of a parish church. The remaining ten were delivered in academic situations. But this last item is not without its implications for parish preaching. As Joseph Sittler has pointed out: "The situation that characterizes the collegiate congregation now, will deepeningly characterize the ordinary parish congregation tomorrow." [2]

To be sure, the institution comes under the word of judgment quite explicitly in Lazareth's "Wanted: Mulatto Salesmen" and in Snook's "The Vision of Pentecost," and implicitly elsewhere. Several of the sermons submitted, but not included here, were obviously written by angry young men frustrated and even embittered by the institution's preoccupation with itself. But there is only questionable value

[2] Joseph Sittler. *The Care of the Earth and Other University Sermons.* (Philadelphia: Fortress Press. 1964). p. 1.

to angry blasts from the pulpit—they may serve to relieve some of the preacher's frustrations, but little more. The *church* comes under the word of judgment here, but the preachers' concerns are directed more to the *world* the church is called to serve than to the plight or the possibilities of the institution as institution. This would seem to indicate a considerable measure of maturity among these younger preachers as well as an awareness of where the vital issues lie.

The sermons grouped under the heading, "The World in an Uproar," are concerned directly with the Christian's involvement in the world. Lazareth, Marty and White are examples of the preacher's concern for the involvement of the congregation in the obvious revolutions going on in the streets of "the secular city." They underline the comment that, if one is not involved in the current struggle for rights and freedom for minority groups, one is not fully alive.

On a broader level, Bosch's "The Seed and the Soils in the Age-After-Christendom," and Vannorsdall's "The Siren Song of Wisdom's Maids" and "Letter Home" reflect what Martin Marty calls "a world of displacement." [3] This is the world in which the contemporary man is constrained to live and move and have his being. Harvey Cox, in discussing the mobility characteristic of "the secular city," declares, "Jahweh was not a place God." [4] In their sermons Bosch and Vannorsdall reflect with unerring accuracy the precise predicament of the displaced Christian. He is not called to find a secure place for himself in the church; he is not bemused by easy solutions for the ambiguities in the world provided by an over-simplified gospel;

[3] *Op. cit.* p. 5.
[4] Harvey Cox. *The Secular City.* (New York: Macmillan. 1965). p. 55.

rather is he called to live in the world of displacement for which Christ died.

Vannorsdall's "Letter Home" is an intriguing example of an oblique approach to a congregation. It raises the question whether the unusual format ought not to be entertained more frequently in the contemporary pulpit. The only difficulty is that the unusual format readily becomes a pulpit gimmick unless the preacher is gifted with imagination and discipline. Note the lack of sentimentality here in a situation where sentimentality lurks around every corner, and the precision with which the family relationships are reflected, providing a context of utter reality in which the problem of the Christian's involvement in the world is exposed in the light of the gospel.

This suggests that the Christian's involvement in the world is set forth not only in the explicit content of the sermon, but also in the style in which the sermon is written. The world is not only outside the four walls of the church in which the sermon is preached; the world is also present in the congregation assembled in the church and in the person of the preacher himself. And one of the tasks of the preacher is to communicate the presence of the world in the way in which he presents his material. This task includes the language he uses, the images, the illustrations, the allusions.

The world is very much present in these sermons. Although there is no embarrassment in the use of biblical language and allusions, the "language of Canaan" is absent. Sometimes the presence of the world is evident in the major images. Note Hoh's use of the soundproof room in a meditation that might be dangerously "otherworldly." See also Bosch's "cup of consecrated chicken soup" in "In Defense of Materialism," Anderson's striking reference to two statues of Rodin, as well as Snook's homely image of his dream of marriage and the home in "The Vision of Pentecost." The alien world in which the people live all the rest of the week except for the sacred hour on Sundays at eleven can be brought into the sacred hour by the selection of major images.

Or it can be done by the language used in the pulpit. Note the brittle facts of city life which White introduces into his "The Office of Shepherd Today." Or, in an entirely different approach, note the creative mixture of traditional and contemporary language in all three of Doan's sermons. See, too, the deceptively simple language in Simonson's "God and Government Glue," Jenson's brief meditation on "Self Control," and Anderson's "Happiness or the Hand of God?" Here we are miles away from the stultifying pulpit language which shuts the world out of the sacred hour for the world is very much present in the way in which the sermon is worded. The language of the sermon is not mere adornment; it can convey the reality of the world outside the church in which the people must live, as well as, of course, the pertinence of the word of God for that world.

A number of these sermons are concerned with what many analysts of the contemporary church call its fixation with the "private" world of the individual; a world always in danger of being cut off from the public world of politics, race relations, corporations, labor unions, and other power structures. But if this private world were the only concern of these sermons, or the sole concern in any given pulpit, then they would indeed be suspect and, perhaps, provide evidence for a lack of renewal in the pulpit.

There is, however, an aspect to the renewal of the church that is frequently missing or, at least, muted in much of the renewal literature. On every hand the church is called to mission, to serve the world, to become a servant church, to lose itself in giving of itself to the revolutionary age. Not often, however, is much attention given to the plight of the individual caught in the throes of rapid change, secularity and revolution. If "the church is mission," whence comes the commitment to mission? Not by a simple call to commitment. Colin Williams, in discussing the problem of anxiety in a world of rapid social change, observes (interestingly enough in a footnote!): "The church must seek to understand how we can speak to the need of man for a basic security from within which he can be free for change." [5]

Precisely here is one of the major functions of the pulpit in the renewal of the church. Obviously there must be explicit references to the Christian's involvement in, and responsibility to, the world. But if this is the primary note in contemporary preaching, then, theologically, the primary note in such preaching is the preaching of the law. When Harvey Cox refers to the gospel as a ". . . summons to leave behind the society and symbols of a dying era and to assume responsibility for devising new ones . . ." [6] he seems to be turning gospel into law. Behind and beneath the summons, the call to commitment, the charge to act responsibly, must be the word of the gospel addressed to the "need of man for a basic security from within which he can be free for change." Of course, if *this* is the only note sounded from the pulpit, then the critics who charge the church with ministering to a truncated private world are right. Gospel and law are always intimately intertwined when a

[5] Colin W. Williams. *What in the World.* (New York: National Council of the Churches of Christ in the USA, 1964). p. 13.
[6] *Op. cit.* p. 117.

sermon reflects the word of God with any degree of accuracy. But surely one of the major emphases in the pulpit at this time of renewal should be its deep involvement in the problems of anxiety, rootlessness and meaninglessness in a world of frighteningly rapid change.

These sermons represent a creative tension between law and gospel and, for the most part, serve to undergird the individual in his struggle to become free for change. Nowhere does this come out more explicitly than in Bosch's fresh treatment of the parable of the seed and the soils. But it is also strongly evident in Luecke's "There's Glory for You," Stuempfle's "The Eye of God," Doan's "A Perspective on the Ascension," and Vannorsdall's "The Shape of Hope."

Nor can these preachers speak to the plight of the displaced person in a secular world unless there is evidence that the preacher himself knows the tensions, the threat of meaninglessness and of despair, and has wrestled with them in the light of the biblical revelation. This note of authenticity comes out clearly in Vannorsdall's "Letter Home," Snook's "The Vision of Pentecost," Nilssen's "He Called Her by Name," and Niedenthal's "Faith: A Posture of Living." It is obvious in these sermons, as well as in others, that whatever "answers" are offered have not hardened. These men report an on-going struggle in which they are themselves deeply involved and their testimony is simply to what they are going through. They know what it means to be displaced. But they also know something more and witness to it. The sheer authenticity of this kind of preaching can do more for renewal in the pulpit than perhaps any other single factor. There is a large place for preaching to the private world of the individual if it carries this kind of stark realism both with respect to contemporary man's predicament and with respect to the kind of security the gospel has to offer.

A third major characteristic of these sermons is the strong emphasis on *didache,* the teaching function of the pulpit. No one of them simply attempts to convey information, of course. They are examples of proclamation. But in, with, and under the proclamation is solid teaching.

It is commonplace to point to the need for solid teaching in the renewal of the church. Biblical illiteracy is an open scandal, and equally scandalous is the lack of understanding of the major doctrinal emphases of the church. And in any significant renewal, the pulpit can do very little in and by itself in meeting these problems. This is the primary function of the educational program in parish or on campus, of Bible study, lay academies, etc. But the pulpit can help to prepare the way.

Consequently, the reader should note well the scrupulous honesty and careful exegesis evident here in the treatment of chosen texts. Note Bosch's handling of the parable of the seed and the soils and the temptation to allegorization, Lazareth's sound treatment of the familiar parable of the Good Samaritan, Snook's wrestling with the account of Pentecost in Acts 2 as well as his carefully documented discussion of angels in "Jesus Was No Angel," Marty's honesty in dealing with Revelation 14, Luecke's rich treatment of the wedding feast at Cana. Biblical illiteracy is too often fed by sloppy and superficial handling of texts in the pulpit. Not so here.

But even more evident in these sermons is the attempt to wrestle with the hard and knotty essentials of the faith. The third group of sermons is actually a series of doctrinal sermons, even though they hardly read that way! Here are sermons that tackle such knotty doctrinal questions as the implications of the ascension, the Lord's Supper, the meaning of faith, the resurrection, the baffling problem of angels and Jesus' secularity, Pentecost, and a brief but deeply perceptive exploration into the meaning of hope.

Theological interest is not limited to the last group of sermons, of course. Note Luecke's exploration into the meaning of glory, Doan's treatment of the Lord's Supper in "Communion and Emotion," the interplay of judgment and redemption in Stuempfle's "The Eye of God," and the perplexing problem of God's activity in the world as it underlies Bosch's "In Defense of Materialism" and Simonson's "God and Government Glue." Indeed, underlying all of the sermons is the theological concern indispensable to creative proclamation.

Some might question the inclusion of Elvee's "When You Are Young You See Things Separately" in this connection. Could not this chapel meditation have been delivered by a rabbi? What is the theological concern evident here? The meditation was included in the collection first because of its haunting beauty and its unusual format. But also, and far more importantly, because it represents an oblique approach to college students. In content it is something less than the gospel; it is pre-evangelical. But because its imagery prods the imagination, it teases and tantalizes and suggests that there is more to be said. And surely on occasion this is a valuable approach to the student mind, or to the secular mind, for that matter.[7]

[7] See Martin Marty's discussion of "presentation" vs. "communication" in connection with the religious use of the mass media in *The Improper Opinion* (Philadelphia: Westminster Press, 1961) pp. 86 ff. The discussion is pertinent for the pulpit as well: "Here is a one way act that sets the terms for later communication . . . the communication known as presentation has a promissory character; it tends to tantalize and to offer more than it can deliver, but what it offers can be honest" (p. 88).

Actually most of the sermons are characterized by the same quality. Langdon Gilkey has said, "The preaching of the minister should be the beginning, not necessarily the end, of discussion." [8] The teaching function of the pulpit in the renewal of the church is severely restricted, to be sure. But if the sermon can open up questions, if it can tantalize and suggest that there is far more to be said, it can creatively motivate the listener to seek further, to enter into discussion and dialogue. In this collection we are offered no closed systems, no easy answers, no dogmatic shutting of doors to further questions. Elvee's delicate and tantalizing approach is actually symptomatic of an essential quality of openness characteristic of the collection as a whole.

One further characteristic of these sermons deserves comment. What of the problem of transcendence in a world where the overwhelming evidence of deep-rooted secularity has called into question even the use of the word, "God." So Harvey Cox writes, "It may well be our English word for God will have to die . . . (and we shall have to) stop talking about 'God' for a while . . . until the new name emerges." [9] Van Buren echoes the same concern: "A straightforward use of the word, 'God', must be abandoned" (even though, as he notes, we continue to take Christianity seriously).[10]

These sermons are not unaware of the problem of secularity, even the "death of God", as witness, e.g., the two sermons by Bosch and Snook's "Jesus Was No Angel." And yet there is no embarrassment at the straightforward

[8] Langdon Gilkey, *How the Church Can Minister to the World Without Losing Itself* (New York: Harper & Row, 1964). p. 82.
[9] *Op. cit.* pp. 265-266.
[10] Paul M. Van Buren. *The Secular Meaning of the Gospel* (New York: Macmillan, 1963). p. 100.

use of the word, God. The problem may be resolved by re-calling that these sermons are not addressed to the "secular man" who is completely divorced from the symbolism of the Bible or who has utterly rejected any view of transcendence which looks "beyond" or "above" this world. The people who heard these sermons were, after all, in church or chapel. The traditional symbols of the faith may well be distorted for them or even empty of meaning. But they are there hopefully looking for new meaning and, perhaps, even the correction of distortions.

Martin Marty has observed: "It is necessary to suggest that whatever unbelief is occurring in the United States—whether of the closed or open variety—it will have to be sought not in overt expressions of atheism and disbelief, but under the symbols of continuity established by organized religious groups, particularly those with historic Christian reference." [11] These sermons use the "symbols of continuity" without embarrassment: God, word of God, Christ, Bible, even angels and the ascension! But always there is an effort to pour new meaning into these symbols in terms of the secularity of the world in which both preacher and congregation live.

Thus, these preachers do not go nearly so far as the more radical exponents of the "secular gospel." The assumption is that "God" is not limited to this world. The resurrection is far more than ". . . the strange story of how (Jesus') freedom became contagious on Easter." [12] The resurrection has to do with death—the ongoing problem of physical death—and what lies beyond. See, e.g., Nilssen's remarkable struggle with this problem in "He Called Her by

[11] Martin E. Marty, *Varieties of Unbelief* (New York: Holt, Rinehart and Winston, 1964). pp. 96-97.
[12] Van Buren, *op. cit.* p. 144.

Name" as well as Niedenthal's "Faith: A Posture of Living."

Perhaps this may mean that these preachers are too "conservative" for any radical renewal of the pulpit in the face of a massively secular age. Or it may mean that while accepting the analysis of our age as to its secularity, they are unwilling to give up the possibility of a "God" who is "beyond" or "above." At least it is evident that they are aware of the problem and are in process of fighting their way through it. Meanwhile they give attention to the biblical "symbols of continuity" in depth and with imagination.

The place of the pulpit in the renewal of the church is no doubt limited. We can find far more dramatic evidence for renewal in biblical theology, the ecumenical movement, the small group movement, lay activity, liturgical revival, involvement in the civil rights struggle, and experimental missions to the inner city. But so long as people gather for worship about the word and the sacraments, proclamation is involved. These sermons are offered as documentation of the fact that renewal in the pulpit can happen and is happening, at least among a younger generation of preachers in America. And this is good news indeed.

EDMUND A. STEIMLE

Union Theological Seminary
New York, New York
Pentecost, 1966

The World

in an Uproar

ONE

The Seed and the Soils in the Age-After-Christendom

PAUL F. BOSCH

And when a great crowd came together and people from town after town came to him, he said in a parable: "A sower went out to sow his seed; and as he sowed, some fell along the path, and was trodden under foot, and the birds of the air devoured it. And some fell on the rock; and as it grew up, it withered away, because it had no moisture. And some fell among thorns; and the thorns grew with it and choked it. And some fell into good soil and grew, and yielded a hundredfold." As he said this, he called out, "He who has ears to hear, let him hear."

And when his disciples asked him what this parable meant, he said, "To you it has been given to know the secrets of the kingdom of God; but for others they are in parables, so that seeing they may not see, and hearing they may not understand. Now the parable is this: The seed is the word of God. The ones along the path are those who have heard; then the devil comes and takes away the word from their hearts, that they may not believe and be saved. And the ones on the rock are those who, when they hear the word, receive it with joy; but these have no root, they

*believe for a while and in time of temptation fall away.
And as for what fell among the thorns, they are those who
hear, but as they go on their way they are choked by the
cares and riches and pleasures of life, and their fruit does
not mature. And as for that in the good soil, they are those
who, hearing the word, hold it fast in an honest and good
heart, and bring forth fruit with patience."*

—Luke 8:4-15

I'D LIKE TO TURN TO THE GOSPEL
for the day, this parable of Jesus about the seed and the
soils, because it illuminates for me the relationship between
the world and the disciple, the message and its hearers. It
tells me something about the success (if you want to use
the term) of religion (if you want to use the term) in the
Post-Christian Era (if you want to use the term). And it
reminds me about the discipline of Christian life, and
speaks a word of warning about what we are to trust and
not to trust.

I read in this parable a sobering word—a word of judgment, on the one hand, and a cheerful word—a word of
grace, on the other.

First the sobering thought, the word of judgment, and
it's downright depressing on your bad days. That is, the
great waste in the religious life and life in general, the
great inefficiency, the overwhelming evidence of tragedy.
Jesus uses here in the eighth chapter of Luke the world of
nature with its seeds and soils as a parable for the world
generally, including the world of the spirit. And he makes
his first point quite clear. The seed is the word of God; the
soils represent its reception. In an age which knew little
about the sophistications of modern agriculture, the sower

sows his seed, and for each scattering that falls on good soil, some falls on the path and some on the rock and some among weeds. The picture at its first impression is clearly one of inefficiency and waste.

Now I'm sure Jesus did not intend that we should draw a precise percentage out of the story as if of all the seed sown, precisely three-fourths was wasted, precisely one-fourth came to fruit. Yet the picture still remains at first a sobering one: an overwhelming evidence of tragedy.

And I believe we'd be making a mistake to allegorize this simple parable, to ask of ourselves or of our neighbors or our churches, "What kind of seed is here?" "What kind of soil . . . ?" As a matter of fact, I believe Luke makes a mistake in allegorizing it, putting those words in the mouth of Jesus which we read in the eleventh to fifteenth verses, explaining, allegorizing the seed on each soil. There's reason to suspect that this allegorizing is not from Jesus' lips, but represents a later elaboration of a simple parable.

At any rate, forget the allegory here. Forget verses eleven to fifteen and concentrate instead on the parable as a whole. Look for the chief message, the chief implications.

And the first of the chief implications is overwhelmingly this: that left to itself the world is a desert; that there is inevitable waste in the witness of truth and in its reception in the hearts of men; an inefficiency—no, more than that—a conspiracy against the growth of what is really good and true; a conspiracy that can only be described as hellish; a conspiracy that in three cases out of four—perhaps in seven cases out of eight—leaves the truth, to change the figure, stillborn and aborted in the delivery room.

Now that's the first point of the parable as I read it, and

4

it's a sobering word, a word of judgment, even of despair: there is waste and tragedy in the world of nature, and also in the world of the spirit. Jesus is reminding us here, twenty centuries in advance, of what Darwin and the evolutionists teach in their doctrines of natural selection: that of all the seeds sown among the trails and weeds and rocks, only a few take root and come to flower. Of perhaps fifteen seedlings planted in a woodlot, after so many years only ten remain, and after so many more years only five, and after so many more years only one.

Now this tells me something about the world and about the place of truth in it. It explains to me the overwhelming evidence of tragedy and waste and unfulfillment. It reminds me that a tragic vision of life is to be found somewhere at the heart of the Christian message; that left to itself, the world is a desert, a wilderness; that left to themselves, events of personal or public history are apt to deteriorate and decay rather than improve; that the bad is the rule, the good the exception.

In another sense, this is simply to recognize the presence of sin (if you want to use the term) in a fallen world (if you want to use the term). I suppose this is also to recognize what some have called the Post-Christian Era, the time after Christendom, and to ask the question, was it ever any different, the world being what it is, namely, three-fourths falling apart? This is also to say something about the death of God in our day and to ask the question, for whom has he really been alive for two thousand or four thousand years, the world in every age being what it is, namely, three-fourths or seven-eighths going to hell?

This is simply to admit that the word of truth has always been since the beginning, and will always be until the end, a minority voice, a minority song in a majority clamor, a minority seed in a majority wilderness. Now if it's any comfort to you who call yourselves religionists, remember this: this is true not only of the gospel, not only of Christianity, but also, I believe, in every area of importance.

I believe we're justified in extending the scope of the parable. The sobering thought is that there's waste all around and tragedy and thwarted promise. The good, the true, the beautiful: these are really rare commodities in our world, the exception. There's much more evidence for the bad, for the false or irrelevant, for the ugly. These commodities are in the vast majority.

It's simply a matter of reading the evidence of experience realistically: most teachers are bad teachers, and if you've had good ones most of your life, you simply don't know how lucky you've been. Most paintings, even in galleries, are bad paintings, inauthentic art. Most novels are bad novels, untrue novels. There's little evidence for the good, the true. Christ is warning his disciples about the dreadful waste and thwarted purpose and tragedy in a fallen world. He's warning against Pollyanna optimism.

Now the implication of this for us is that there's a tremendous work to be done. If there is such a suffocating waste in the world, such a conspiracy of tragedy and evil, then someone had better sow the seed and sow it recklessly and widely. This seed that fell on good ground: it may well be only one-quarter of the total sown or less, yet it's only here that any hope resides. If three-quarters of the seed is stillborn and aborted, then there's a tremendous job to be done by the one-quarter left, that tiny proportion that grows to full maturity.

I suppose, to be perfectly honest—and to extend my

analogy to its limit—this means you can't expect to get much good out of three-quarters of the sermons you hear including, I suppose, this one. And again, to be perfectly honest—and to extend the analogy to its limits—it means I shouldn't expect anything out of three-quarters of you: I should expect three-quarters of you to miss the point, or perhaps to get the point and be offended by it, or perhaps three-quarters of you are simply asleep this morning.

At any rate, all this simply serves to remind me of the Old Testament's understanding of the remnant, an understanding which seems to many to be especially relevant in the twentieth century. Only a remnant, only a minority can be counted on in the crisis.

So Christ cries at the end of his parable: "He who has ears to hear, let him hear." And to that small minority band of disciples he says, "To you it has been given to know the secrets of the kingdom of God; but for others . . ."—that vast and heathen majority—"for others they are in parables, so that seeing they may not see, and hearing they may not understand."

Luke makes a point of reporting that people came in large numbers—a great crowd—to hear Jesus, but only the disciples are made to understand. I'm sure that as a conscious literary artist, Luke meant the parallel to be quite clear: the great crowds of people a parallel for the unproductive soils along the pathways, among the weeds and rocks; the small remnant-number of disciples a parallel for the productive soil, where the seed grows to full maturity and brings forth fruit with patience.

Now discipleship in this kind of a minority, this kind of a remnant, will not be easy. We're simply not a mighty army, those of us who name Christ's name. Just look around you this morning if you want depressing evidence of that. And the burden of discipleship under such circumstances will be a tough one.

The fact is that Christ doesn't expect anything of the majority, the three-quarters of seed that fell by the wayside or among the weeds and rocks. He does expect it of you, you few who are willing to respond. Christ sometimes seems to be especially tough with his disciples, demanding more of them than of others. This is probably the point of the parable of the laborers in the vineyard—the parable about those who worked through the heat and burden of the day and then could claim no special favor over those who worked an hour.

Jesus is simply giving notice that he expects more of the good seed, the good soil. And rightly so! Who else? Surely not the others—that mighty army of unproductives? If we are indeed entering an era which is "post-Christendom," when for many God is dead, then it simply means an extra burden on those for whom he is alive. We may not always see the results, the harvest. We may not have proof in this life of a final victory or even of the relevance of the fight. We may be called upon, those of us in minority number, to bear the burdens of a multitude. And yet we must still sow recklessly and widely, cultivating and cherishing those rare instances, those rare evidences of truth and beauty and goodness all the while harboring, in a sense, a tragic vision of life, not kidding ourselves that anything we do will make a huge difference or convert the world overnight to Utopia.

It's a sobering word here, a word of judgment and warning to the few, the remnant, a word not offering them escape from heavy responsibility or from suffering.

Now there's a cheerful word here too, a word of grace, and for me it makes all the difference. This is the tremendous potency of the little good there is when empowered by God's word.

This is for me a word of exhilarating cheerfulness, and it allows me to talk at times about the world going to hell, meaning it quite literally yet with a certain good-humor, if not flippancy. This is the cheerful promise of the proclamation of total victory, a harvest rich and full and complete in spite of desert, in spite of weeds, in spite of rock.

This exhilarating promise, this cheerful word that all is grace—it does not make the first part of the parable, the sobering part, any less true or any less sobering. It simply makes it more bearable. As a matter of fact, for me it makes life bearable, and without it, I think I'd go home and turn on the gas burners. This is the thrilling assurance, the eschatological assurance, that God in Christ has once for all sown a seed, and that seed will bear fruit positively, absolutely, irrevocably, giving increase beyond measure.

This tells me something about the potency of the word of truth. It may not be efficient by the standards of the world. It may mean a remnant, a minority who stand and serve and suffer for the majority. Nevertheless the chief point is this: the word does work. It has success. It is productive thirty-fold and sixty-fold and one hundred-fold.

Christ here also reminds his disciples of this second fact: this proclamation of grace; the potency of his word which does what it says; the increase of the good to the fulfillment of his purposes. Now that's a promise of reward. It's a promise, a proclamation of victory which I take to be nothing less than total victory in spite of every obstacle.

I have no doubt that this parable is to be interpreted in the light of Isaiah 55. I'm sure Jesus had precisely this prophecy in mind in telling his story:

> "For as the rain and the snow come down from heaven,
>   and return not thither but water the earth,
>   making it bring forth and sprout,
>   giving seed to the sower and bread to the eater,
>   so shall my word be that goes forth from my mouth;
>   it shall not return to me empty,
>   but it shall accomplish that which I purpose,
>   and prosper in the thing for which I sent it.
>
> "For you shall go out in joy,
>   and be led forth in peace;
>   the mountains and the hills before you shall break forth
>   into singing
>   and all the trees of the field shall clap their hands.
>   Instead of the thorn shall come up the cypress;
>   instead of the brier shall come up the myrtle;
>   and it shall be to the Lord for a memorial,
>   for an everlasting sign which shall not be cut off."
>   (Isaiah 55:10-13)

This is an eschatological assurance. That is, it points to God's creative and re-creative activity beyond history and within it; an activity which moves history towards its end which is also its consummation, the glorious fulfillment of its purpose; a victory, a fulfillment, a completion in which the whole creation shares, in which I share, and you; an assurance that that victory, once begun in Christ, will be completed to magnificent all-encompassing fullness.

The seed is an immensely suggestive image here: a

round, brown husk having in itself no life, no vital juices pulsing through its cells, not a living, growing plant, but —wonder of wonders!—not a stone either, but pregnant with life, vibrant life, needing only the fulness of time, and then, magnificent increase thirty-fold, sixty-fold, one hundred-fold!

Most often this text is used to remind Christians of their own witness, the place of the religious enterprise. And it's an especially welcome, cheerful word in our Post-Christendom world; the reminder that if we few, the minority, sow God's word widely and well, with extravagance, with recklessness, then in the fulness of time God will grant the increase. It's a reminder that Post-Christian times will not necessarily be bad times, but, perhaps, good times for the word, for the gospel, pregnant with promise.

And so the disciple enters this era of history as he enters every era, sitting loose in the saddle, so to speak. He doesn't "sweat it." The religious enterprise, the witness of the truth of the gospel, is by no means doomed. It will accomplish. It will succeed.

But beyond that assurance looms an even more cosmic hope, brilliant with promise, that the fulness of God's creative grace and power and authority slumbers in his world, as in his word, and it will not return void or empty, but full. It's the promise that all bad will one day be good, all falsehood and irrelevance one day truth, all fractured ugliness one day beauty. The eleventh-hour laborer will receive his wage too, along with him who bore the heat of the day.

And believe it or not, there's evidence for this hope, hints and types and parables of this word of grace to be found in the world around us. So, for instance, in the sci-

11

ences we stand on the threshold of new control over our environment, new mastery over our powers and the powers of the universe. And in the arts, sculptures and paintings of great beauty and sensitivity made entirely from junk, the castoffs of our waste reclaimed and redeemed. I like the image of a church being built with cinder blocks and pressurized sawdust! And in medicine, surgery that makes our previous miracles of surgery look crude. Have you heard about the electronic ear installed in a woman's head? Not a hearing aid but an ear, as I have it, sending impulses to the auditory nerves.

These are themselves parables, signs, types of the harvest that is to come. It's a reminder to the disciple that on occasion the world may be going to hell—but not permanently, not finally. It's a reminder that he must work like the devil, that is, like the devil works, with all his hellish energies as part of only the smallest minority—and yet, it doesn't depend ultimately on him. It's the promise that the success of the word does not depend on waste or on tragedy, or on majority numbers, nor less yet on our own imperfect discipleship—but rather on its own inner authority, its own transforming power, to accomplish that which it says.

We can dare to look around us with cheerfulness, catching glimpses and previews of the day of the increase of the seed when this desert, this wilderness of a world, becomes once again a garden according to God's promise.

TWO

Wanted:
Mulatto Salesmen

WILLIAM H. LAZARETH

And behold, a lawyer stood up to put him to the test, saying, "Teacher, what shall I do to inherit eternal life?" He said to him, "What is written in the law? How do you read?" And he answered, "You shall love the Lord your God with all your heart, and with all your soul, and with all your strength, and with all your mind; and your neighbor as yourself." And he said to him, "You have answered right; do this, and you will live."

But he, desiring to justify himself, said to Jesus, "And who is my neighbor?" Jesus replied, "A man was going down from Jerusalem to Jericho, and he fell among robbers, who stripped him and beat him, and departed, leaving him half dead. Now by chance a priest was going down that road; and when he saw him he passed by on the other side. So likewise a Levite, when he came to the place and saw him, passed by on the other side. But a Samaritan, as he journeyed, came to where he was; and when he saw him, he had compassion, and went to him and bound up his wounds, pouring on oil and wine; then he set him on his own beast and brought him to an inn,

*and took care of him. And the next day he took out two
denarii and gave them to the innkeeper, saying, 'Take care
of him; and whatever more you spend, I will repay you
when I come back.' Which of these three, do you think,
proved neighbor to the man who fell among the robbers?"
He said, "The one who showed mercy on him." And Jesus
said to him, "Go and do likewise."*

—*Luke* 10:25-37

THERE ARE TWO EXPLOSIVE
revolutions going on in America today. The one is religious, and the other is racial. Both struggles involve you as
a Christian and as an American. Sooner or later, every one
of you is going to have to stand and be counted.

The religious revolution is out to destroy the second-class citizenship of laymen in our churches. After centuries
of broken promises by condescending clergymen, laymen
finally want their "responsibility now!" Believing Martin
Luther, they are sure that there must be more to Christian
discipleship than just sitting quietly in the back pews of
their own churches.

The racial revolution is determined to eliminate the
second-class citizenship of Negroes in our society. After
centuries of broken promises by condescending white men,
Negroes are impatiently demanding their "freedom now!"
Believing Martin Luther King, they are certain that there
must be more to American citizenship than just sitting
quietly in the back seats of their own buses.

Both religiously and racially, American Christians have
reached the point of no return. We cannot turn back the
clock. Our lives will never again be the same, either inside
or outside the walls of the church. Those old walls are

14

crumbling and traditional patterns are dying. Time-honored customs are being flaunted by loyal pillars of the church, as well as by foolish extremists. Unjust laws are being broken by respected leaders in the community, as well as by dangerous fanatics. Desperately in need of divine guidance, we turn obediently to the judging and merciful word of God.

Happily, our text this morning deals with Christ's explanation of God's law of love in his parable of the good Samaritan. Our Lord's words are as timely as this morning's newspaper. They are bitingly relevant to the crises in our church and community life. What about shirt-sleeve evangelism and witnessing on the job? How about color-blind ministries and desegregated classrooms? All these current challenges in religion and race fall quickly into place once we are constrained by the love of Christ to re-enact the neighborliness of the good Samaritan right here on the streets of downtown Pittsburgh. But, first, let us look more deeply into the biblical witness itself.

I

"Teacher, what shall I do to inherit eternal life?" This is the question posed by a probing lawyer "to put him to the test." Jesus is being challenged as a teacher, as a rabbi, on his interpretation of the value of the law of Israel for man's salvation. Meeting the lawyer on his own grounds, Jesus quickly parries the question with another one: "What is written in the law?"

The lawyer answers, "You shall love the Lord your God with all your heart, and with all your soul, and with all your strength, and with all your mind; and your neighbor as yourself." Jesus is obviously pleased with the lawyer's summary of the divine law in terms of man's two-fold love of God and neighbor. He responds at once, "You have answered right; do this, and you will live."

We would do well to pause here a moment to make sure that we have grasped the full meaning of this brief but profound exchange. Jesus is affirming that love—and love alone—is able to fulfill the law of God. Love marks the end of the law, both as its goal and as its finish.

Pious Jews in Jesus' day were expected to obey some six hundred thirteen religious commandments which tried to legislate every last detail of their civil, moral, and ceremonial duties. Men were ordered when to pray, what to eat, where to travel, how to farm, when to fish, and whom to obey. With so many impersonal rules, people gradually lost touch with their personal ruler. The love of law crowded out the law of love. *What* was done became more important than *why* it was done. Men's hands were clean, but their hearts were corrupt. Jesus condemned them as "whitewashed tombs"—spotless on the outside, but full of dead bones on the inside.

In opposition to all this loveless legalism, Jesus insists that our character determines our conduct, our motives shape our deeds. This is true because we are all created in the image of a holy and loving God. Our capacity to live in love—with God and with each other—is the distinctive mark of our humanity. To be unloving is to be inhuman. If men want to inherit eternal life, that is, life in communion with the eternal God of love, then they must obey the only demand that he makes of his beloved creatures: they must freely share with their neighbors that same love which he freely showers upon them.

This means, in practical terms, that the actual needs of

our flesh-and-blood neighbors are far more important than any abstract moral principles or inflexible legal ordinances. Jesus declared, "The sabbath was made for man, not man for the sabbath." In fact, healing on the sabbath against the law was Jesus' way of showing that loveless laws must bow to loving persons whenever the two come into conflict.

Paul proclaimed that same law-free gospel. "Owe no one anything, except to love one another; for he who loves his neighbor has fulfilled the law." Centuries later, Luther, in *The Small Catechism,* likewise prefaced every one of his explanations of the Ten Commandments with an identical love-centered motive: "We are to fear and love God so that we do not . . ." curse, kill, seduce, steal, slander, or covet all that rightly belongs to our needy neighbors.

This law of love—"service above and beyond the call of duty"—is a hard rule for men to live by, especially when they are by nature as unloving as you and I. "Love your neighbor" seems so vague, so general, so all-inclusive. Instinctively we yearn to pin it down, box it up, spell it out. If only our "neighbors" could be identified, localized, maybe even codified, then the love commandment might be made manageable, reasonable and, perhaps, even practicable.

This is why the calculating lawyer in each of our hearts demands of Jesus, "And *who* is my neighbor?" That is, just how many of these needy "cases"—a, b, c, d,—am I expected to serve? Tell me, Jesus, just which "classifications" of men deserve my loving care—and, equally important, which of them do not?

At this crucial point Jesus tries to lead the lawyer to a far deeper awareness of what neighborly love is all about. He tells him a parable about a man who is robbed, beaten,

17

and left to die. First a priest and then a Levite refuse to come to his aid, and pass him by on the other side. Finally a Samaritan comes along who shows compassion on him. He goes out of his way to help, first by dressing the victim's wounds, and then by arranging for his further care at a nearby inn.

On face value this parable is so deceptively simple that even a small child could draw the obvious moral conclusion: "Of course! Your neighbor is anyone who needs your help." But Jesus does not permit the lawyer to substitute moralism for legalism as in one of Aesop's little fables. No, our Lord wants to show the lawer that the moral problems he has are due to the religious problem he is. An unloving man is always his own worst enemy. He needs help not to find, but to become, the right kind of neighbor.

Therefore Jesus prods the lawyer to examine his own heart by asking: "Which of these three *proved* to be a neighbor in this situation?" "The one who showed mercy on him" is now the only possible answer. But note well: it is also an answer which demands a radical reversal in the lawyer's whole ethical outlook. To fulfill God's law of love, the right question is not, "Who is my neighbor?" but rather, "Whose neighbor am I?" The Samaritan loves because he is loving, not because the victim is lovable. Being a neighbor, the Samaritan naturally acts neighborly. So having seared our consciences with the Samaritan's unselfish example, Jesus admonishes the lawyer in each of us to "go and do likewise."

II

When it comes to practicing God's law of love in the homes and schools and stores of downtown Pittsburgh, I'm sure that there was one feature in Jesus' parable which none of you missed: the good Samaritan was a layman. In other words, the hero of one of our Lord's most poignant parables was not a "professional clergyman in full-time Christian service." This is of great importance for that remarkable recovery of the ministry of the laity occurring throughout so many of our vibrant churches today.

From an evangelical point of view, one of the chief ways in which late Judaism betrayed the covenant faith of the Old Testament was by permitting a radical divorce to take place between the "priests and Levites" on the one side and the ordinary laymen on the other. We recall that just before God renewed his covenant with Israel atop Mt. Sinai, he reminded Moses of its divine purpose: "Now therefore, if you will obey my voice and keep my covenant . . . you shall be to me a kingdom of priests and a holy nation" (Exodus 19:5-6). Centuries later, after Christ died and rose as "the mediator of a new covenant," the writers of the New Testament likewise described the mission of the church in terms of the faithful and loving priesthood of all those baptized into the body of Christ.

Let's nail this one down hard: any absolute division of the people of God into first and second-class members, one percent of whom are praised as "professional clergymen" while the other ninety-nine percent are only tolerated as "amateur laymen," is a dangerous perversion of the Christian faith. In the first place, there is not even a New Testament word for "clergyman." In the second place, there is no such thing as disciples being called for "part-time Christian service." And in the third place, all baptized Christians are equally "laymen"—the people of God—a few of whom are called to serve Christ's church as his ordained

19

pastors, all of whom are called to serve God's world as his lay priests.

This biblical vision of the ministry of the whole laity of God is once again catching fire in a glorious way throughout the church today. Certainly it was badly needed. After Luther had so strongly stressed the church's "universal priesthood," a new bureaucracy of "priests and Levites" soon re-emerged in the Lutheran state churches of Germany and Scandinavia. But now the twentieth century has challenged all of that. Confronted by an over-secularized world and disenchanted with an over-institutionalized church, more and more Christian laymen are beginning to realize that they are the church at work in and for the world. The church is not some dead building; it is the living body of Christ whose members alternately gather for worship and scatter for service throughout the whole of life.

This shared ministry of the "communion of saints"—pastor and people together—is strongly emphasized by the author of Ephesians. He writes, "And these were his gifts: some to be apostles, some prophets, some evangelists, some pastors and teachers, to equip God's people for work in his service, to the building up of the body of Christ" (4:11-12, NEB). This, then, is the pastor's unique function—"to equip God's people for work in his service." It is as your "enabler" that the pastor fulfills his crucial share of the church's common ministry. He's the coach in the gym; you're the halfback on the world's playing fields. He's the drill sergeant in the boot camp; you're the artilleryman on the world's battlefields. In short, he serves you in the church to equip you to serve others in the world.

Closely related to all this is a second, somewhat more

subtle feature of Christ's parable which may have escaped you. The good Samaritan was not only a layman: he was also a racial outcast. The Samaritans were the despised offspring which issued from the forbidden intermarriages between the Jews and the Arabs. They were persecuted as "mongrels" and segregated as "half-breeds" by the ancient Semitic equivalents of the White Citizens' Councils on both sides of their borders.

In other words, our Lord could hardly have chosen a more controversial figure for the hero of his parable. In terms of a contemporary American parallel, Jesus deliberately illustrates God's holy law of love by praising the lay ministry of a mulatto salesman!

The plight of the Samaritans illustrates a second way in which late Judaism betrayed the covenant faith of the Old Testament. The Jews succumbed to the proud view that they had some special status in God's sight as his chosen people. Prophets like Amos and Jeremiah tried vainly to remind them that God had set his people apart for special service and sacrifice. But the Jews—unfaithful to their holy calling—tried to evade their obedience to God by hiding behind his law within his temple. It took the fall of Israel and Judah to convince them that it did no good simply to pay lip service to the divine law of love. A righteous God would not be mocked by unrighteous men.

In more recent times, many Americans have held the similar view that they were somehow God's newly chosen people. After exploiting the endless resources of a virgin wilderness, prosperous men often came to the blasphemous notion that it was somehow their "manifest destiny" to be specially blessed by God. Long after a bloody civil war was fought and won to eradicate the evils of human slavery from our shores, many Americans still deluded themselves into believing that it was their superior "white man's burden" to impose the "American way of life" on the more backward, less favored, "unchosen" peoples of the world. The so-called "WASPS"—white, Anglo-Saxon, Protestants—tried to recreate mankind according to their own sin-corrupted image.

All this racial idolatry has been brought to a screeching halt in our day. A colored revolution has been taking place throughout the liberated nations of Asia and Africa. At the same time the American non-violent resistance movement has also moved forward with courageous determination.

As democratic Americans, Negroes have rightly challenged unjust laws and social customs that conflict with the constitutional law of the land. Then, going the "second mile" as American Christians, they have also rightly subjected the constitutional law of men to the moral law of God. Courageous Negroes have overcome our heinous church bombings, our degrading fire hoses, and our snarling police dogs, with signs on their backs, hymns on their lips, and prayers in their hearts.

In the presence of Almighty God let us be brutally honest with ourselves this morning. White Christians like you and me have probably also been saved from sure death lately on one of the side streets of Pittsburgh. And, as in Christ's parable, we too, could never begin to repay what we owe to the compassionate "mulatto salesman" ministering among us. Our repentant hearts should be filled with gratitude that centuries of humiliating prejudice, slavery and segregation have not so embittered our Negro neighbors and brothers that they would also—understandably!—pass us by on the other side of the road.

22

Only a small handful of America's colored "priests and Levites" are resorting to the deplorable "blue-eyed white devil" racism of the Black Muslims. Certainly no naive prejudice-in-reverse should now prevent us from condemning their savage riots and lawless fanaticism in the name of God's righteous law. Happily, however, the vast majority of American Negroes are following conscientious Christian leaders in their non-violent struggles for political freedom, economic justice, and social equality.

By way of conclusion, let there be no mistake about where the Lutheran Church in America stands in this critical area of race relations. We believe and teach that the biblical witness is clear and unequivocal: the ever-changing races of men are wholly irrelevant to the never-changing grace of God. In Christ there is neither Jew nor Greek, slave nor free . . . black nor white.

This means that a Christian ministry of love and justice in racially-mixed Pittsburgh should and will result in integrated churches serving desegregated communities. Christ has called us into his universal priesthood to work for man's universal brotherhood under God's universal fatherhood. Let us therefore support every fellow citizen seeking freedom and civil rights to find color-blind justice in an open society. Let us likewise aid every fellow sinner seeking forgiveness and new life to find color-blind fellowship in an open church. And as twentieth century "good Samaritans," let us pray and work together for cities of brotherly love—whether these "Philadelphias" are located in critical Mississippi or in hypocritical Pennsylvania.

In a recent letter addressed to all pastors of the Lutheran Church in America, President Franklin Clark Fry asks the same burning question as Jesus: "Whose neighbor are

23

you?" He declares, "The position that Christians take on race has spiritual roots. It arises directly out of our view of God and of man; and belongs to the essence of our faith. It is accusingly simple and brooks no disagreement.

"Men, created by God and redeemed by Christ, are equals and meant to be brothers. No man is a hair's breadth above or below another in God's affection, nor can he be in a Christian's regard. Any disabilities on the basis of race in the Christian family are evil. They are an affront to the Lord and a sign of deviation from him."

Dr. Fry concludes his letter, "We all agree on this. The time has come to act." Jesus concludes his parable, "Go and do likewise." As a minister of the church of Christ and by his authority, dare I urge less?

THREE

The World in an Uproar

MARTIN E. MARTY

REFORMATION DAY

Then I saw another angel flying in midheaven, with an eternal gospel to proclaim to those who dwell on earth, to every nation and tribe and tongue and people; and he said with a loud voice, "Fear God and give him glory, for the hour of his judgment has come; and worship him who made heaven and earth, the sea and the fountains of water."

—Revelation 14:6-7

The most permanent fate of God's word is that for its sake the world is put into uproar. For the sermon of God comes in order to change and revive the whole earth to the extent that it reaches it.

—Luther, W.A. XVIII, 626

DEAR FRIENDS:

LONG AGO, VERY LONG AGO, *indeed* long ago, God's people had less difficulty imagining the midheaven peopled with flying angels. Long ago they heard them speaking. A troubled young church was given to seeing visions and hearing prophecy: this day we hear of such an example. It falls strangely on our ears. We do not see, do not hear what they saw and heard. Our poet can say:

> The old component parts will stick together
> a decade or so, but O where are the few
>
> rapt intrepid molecules of faith
> that moved the Himalayas of our past,
> that wired the winds for sound and sowed the stars
> with apes and angels?[1]

Less long ago, but still long enough ago to cause us difficulty, some of God's people took one Biblical text about an angel in midheaven, the one we hear today, and applied it to one man who belonged very much to midearth and who had his feet very much on its ground. One party of sixteenth century Germans listened to the dream language of Revelation 14:6-7 and thought they heard in it the prophecy that one day someone like Martin Luther would preach an eternal gospel and throw the world into an uproar with it. They were so sure of the way they applied the biblical text that some of them even used it as the Epistle for the Festival of the Reformation.

As time passed the text came under a cloud. Two-thirds of the Lutheran churches in our nation no longer read this Epistle this day, and few who are in the other one-third preach on it or hear it detailed. An excellent recent book on the preaching of the Epistles of the church year says:

[1] From "The Park at Evening" reprinted from *The Prodigal Never Returns*, by permission of Farrar, Straus & Giroux, Inc. Copyright 1947 by Hugh Chisholm.

"This text appears to lend itself poorly as basis for a sermon. The message of the angel is gospel, but it is the gospel in the form it takes when the hour of judgment has set in."

Why has this text suffered such a fate of neglect? Why are we embarrassed to hear it read or preached? What kind of halitosis or other offense keeps us all at a safe distance? The reasons are many and obvious. First, we are less confident about applying the words of Biblical prophecy to specific people of later times. We know that our forefathers were wrong in connecting this angel with the man who took part in reforming the church. Second, we are uneasy because such a use of a text might add to some sort of cult of a man, and our worship is devoted to the worship of God. But must we so easily abandon the text, and let it lie in the musty confines of a dusty closed book? Must it litter the shelves of librarians and be an object of curiosity only to those who write about the history of the church year?

It has often been our experience that the most embarrassing, the most offensive texts have the most to say to us. We may neglect or bury this word from the dream language of the young church in the last book of the Bible, not because it is so remote and strange, but because it is too direct, too pointed. We must admit the difficulties of the text as evidence against it. For example, the writer speaks of the angel carrying an eternal gospel. But, as one commentator puts it, "the substance of his proclamation is not much of a gospel, and the prophet evidently does not look for much result, if any." We are accustomed to speaking of gospel only as the healing, comforting word wherein God speaks to us of grace in Jesus Christ. Our angel

27

bluntly speaks only of a creating God and then blurts everything out for us in the simple command: "Fear God and give him glory . . . and worship him." This is coupled with a warning that is not gospel to us: "The hour of his judgment has come." This may be the language of the cross, but it comes from the shadow side, the troublous darkened side of the cross.

Perhaps we can receive a clue about interpreting and applying the words if we compare them to something Luther once said about the word of God. (If we cannot compare the *angel* of the text to Luther, we can at least find coincidence in what *both said!*) In one of his debates the reformer claimed: "the most permanent fate of God's word is that for its sake the world is put into uproar. For the sermon of God comes in order to change and revive the whole earth to the extent that it reaches it." Logically, we might turn this around then and say: if words—even words from a pulpit—do not somehow find the world "put into uproar," they do not represent God's word. And if the sermon of man does not somehow change and revive the whole earth to the extent that it reaches it, it must have been only the sermon of man and is not the sermon of God.

Man cannot, of course, produce God. He cannot dangle God like a puppet on a string. He cannot use God as a ventriloquist uses a marionette, to get God to mouth what he wants. He cannot render God audible; he can only help men to hear when God, in his freedom and grace, chooses to speak. So we cannot always produce uproar, change, revival—in short we cannot always reform the church. But we can be alert to hear should God want to cause an uproar with his word, his sermon.

If we keep that in mind, this strange text does begin to speak to us. Today, again, the church experiences judgment along with the world. Today, again, it needs the command to fear God for it more readily seeks to please man than to fear God. Today, again, it must be told to worship the creator and not to be lost in fondling his creatures. Today, again, the church must dream and find itself awaking to new hope. Today we can listen to what this eternal word says specifically to us and our time, and especially concerning those matters which are most on our minds. I shall do my best honestly to locate these matters.

I know the hazards of such a task. As soon as I speak it may sound to the congregation as if I am propagandizing and not preaching; that I have a hidden agenda to unload and am using the occasion. I may fail. Yet each of us must begin somewhere.

What are the preoccupations of the church in the world today? Where is the uproar in the world today? Where is there change and reviving going on? If you each had a pad of paper and were asked to put down the two clusters of events which appeared most often in the newspapers and in your thoughts and conversations this year, matters which were affected by the word of God, I have no doubt that the same two would be on every one's sheet: one, the racial revolution and the part of the churches; two, the renewal and reform spoken of as occurring in Roman Catholicism. If we thought further, I am sure that each of us would also soon be jotting down something about the word in our immediate world, as in our parishes, and finally in our persons. Let us take the word which the Book of Revelation records as falling from an angel's lips and apply it to these four 'uproars' in our world.

I

The hour of God's judgment has come upon us and our nation; the world is put into uproar in the racial revolution of our summers past and in the seasons that are with us.

Not one day did your newspaper or television let you forget the events of this revolution. All of you found yourselves taking a stand, hardening your prejudices or examining your consciences. Of uproar there was plenty. The beast of violence was turned loose in the streets. We who were accustomed to the language of reason or ballot box found we had to cope with revolution and protest, with demonstration and agitation. A frustrated element in our population denied other means of expressing its heart was involved in causing uproar.

These were the years when little girls could march off to Sunday school and be bombed there by those who hit their real target when they bombed the face of Jesus in the stained glass window. These were the years when churchmen participated among the hundreds of thousands who sang of freedom in our nation's capital. These were the years when Christians, often belatedly, took a place of leadership in a movement which—without such leadership —could turn permanently against the Christ of the church. These were the years when, if you were a Methodist of the wrong color in the wrong city, you would be arrested for going to a Methodist church. These were the years when Lutherans had to scurry back to the word of God and do some long overdue homework and then hurry forward to their congregations' practices to make some changes. It is not my purpose to analyze the movement in detail or to bless its every form. *All* events among men must stand

30

under God's judgment as must both sides in this revolution. But it is my purpose to ask whether the word of God has been heard in the uproar.

Who cares, in this context, whether some of our sermons have to be preached by court justices or pressure groups, whether the church was follower or leader? Now we care only of present and future: how responsive are we *now* to the word of God? How responsible are we *now* to the task of stewardship given us who want to listen? How better can we end excess and violence, demonstrations and unreason than to remove their causes? How better to do this than to listen to our text and the bold message its messenger gives us?

Is there not a clue tucked into its angelic word? The God who judges, whose hour has come, who is to be feared and gloried and worshipped, is described in a simple theistic statement as the one who made heaven and earth. Is it not true that we are in trouble because we have all forgotten our creaturehood, our dependency upon God; that we have despised the creaturehood of others who *do* fear God and give him glory? People used to sing:

Earth might be fair, and all men glad and wise . . .
Would man but wake from out his haunted sleep.
Earth will be fair, and all her people one . . .

But her people are not now one, and she is not fair. Her cities are made ugly and unlovely and violent. God who created all is now exercising his right to judge all. Those who, in the tradition of Martin Luther, want to be alert to the uproar God's word causes have to be ready for the change and revival it would bring to the whole earth.

I will offer you two simple tests. If this year you said,

31

"These demonstrations cannot work, for you must change hearts," were you looking only to quiet the uproar or to remove its cause? Was your heart changed? If this year you complained, "They want to legislate morality, but that will not work. You must change people," did you follow what you said must happen? Did you change?

Several years ago in Chicago a young white Christian said to a conference on religion and race, "It is too late. The most creative thing we can do is sit on the curbstone and weep." He sounded almost like the angel of our text: late, urgent, regretful, strident, almost frantic. He sounded almost like the angel, but not quite. Late as matters were, the angel had a plan: he had an eternal gospel and a command.

II

If you asked people about reformation in the church today; if you asked them where change and reviving is going on; if they took their opinions from a reading of the public press, what would they answer? The churches of the reformation, the protesting or Protestant churches know where reform and protest, revival and change should be going on and where such uproar associated with the word of God should be going on. I really do not think that there would be one disagreement in this room, however, as to where people would locate the 'uproar': They would all cite the Roman Catholic ecumenical council, Vatican II, and its discussion of reform. The most noted Protestant theologian in the world has bluntly asked: Are Catholics leaving us behind in reform?

I shall leave it a question. Perhaps the public press gives the wrong picture. Certainly the returns are not all in. Per-

32

haps the final results of the Council are too confusing for us to interpret much. Perhaps there is illusion and delusion. Many of you may have different ideas about this. But I ask you: is there not on the front page of the papers a regular discussion of a church and world under judgment, an eternal word being debated, a command to fear God being heard, and even—whispered now and then—from Rome itself the word, "We did wrong. We are sorry."? It need be only a whisper; we heard nothing at all in this line for four centuries. So a whisper is news, but it is good news. Not that we are in a position to congratulate or condemn another element in the church. Rather, we are in a position to see another element stand under "the hour of God's judgment." If there must be competition, let it be over the issue of who shall most change and be revived! But if Roman Christians are seeking and finding new ways to fear God and give him glory and worship him; if the churches of the Reformation can participate and contribute to the uproar in the world, then we can rejoice even as we reserve judgments. And we can hear the messenger of Revelation 14 speak to us of re-creation in our churches!

III

The racial revolution and reform in the church are great public acts. Yet not all life is lived in the public realm. So if I asked you whether change or reviving is going on, many of you would bear quiet testimony to what goes on in your own parishes.

Sometimes we grow discouraged. Often the only uproar we hear in our congregations is between factions in the Women's Guild; sometimes the fear we know is not fear of God, but fear of offending some social group in the church. Sometimes we worship not him who made heaven and earth, but we worship little bits of silver and copper we have salvaged from the earth. Some will say our parishes are so organized that they make it more difficult, not easier, to hear the eternal gospel or to share in proclaiming it because the "four corners of the earth," the nations and tribes and tongues are screened from view in our cozy church parlors. Sometimes we speak only men's words, but we use holy tones and make these sound like God's words.

Others of you will not find this borne out in your experience. A faithful pastor preaches the word and it is a judgment on your life. He causes uproar in your hearts, an uproar which is quieted only by Christ's healing message. You minister to each other in fellowship and move from the shadow-side to the brightly lit side of the cross of Jesus. You study the Bible and the bewildering world around you and you seek reviving and change. In many of your communities your congregation is not just a huddle of like-minded people of one social class. It is a witness to the fact that some would fear God and give him glory, that in his hour of judgment you would worship the maker.

Each week when you are in range of the "sermon of God" ask how you are involved in its permanent fate. If it does not work to reform you, if it does not work to cause a radical rearrangement of your life, has it been preached and taught? Have you been inattentive? Have you heard? Could the "angel in midheaven" be speaking, with the old urgency, to you and your parish?

IV

I have made escape easy for all of you. I have spoken of events in another part of the country or another part of town or—worse yet—in Rome. Or I have referred to the parish, in which you play a small part. What about you? While the poet Robert Frost is distorting and not saying all that is to be said, he has something to say to us when he writes:

> I bid you to a one man revolution—
> The only kind that is coming.[2]

Finally, the angelic word moves through nations and tribes and tongues and people and comes to you. The loud voice tells you to fear God and give him glory and worship him. You are told of an hour of judgment before the Creator.

Are our embarrassing text and our uncongenial angel really far from the urgency of Jesus' own first and basic message: "The time is fulfilled, and the kingdom of God is at hand; repent, and believe in the gospel" (Mark 1:15). Is the dream doing more than enlarging the directions in which he walked, for "he went about all Galilee, teaching in their synagogues and preaching the gospel of the kingdom and healing every disease and every infirmity among the people" (Matt. 4:23)? Is the bald command of the angel to fear the Creator contradicting what we have heard from the church's great preacher, Paul and his companion? We "bring you good news, that you should turn from these vain things to a living God who made the heaven and the earth and the sea and all that is in them" (Acts 14:15)?

If there has been no uproar when you were confronted with the word, you must ask yourself: was I too apathetic,

[2] From "Build Soil" from *Complete Poems of Robert Frost.* Copyright 1936 by Robert Frost. Copyright © 1964 by Lesley Frost Ballantine. Reprinted by permission of Holt, Rinehart and Winston, Inc.

too preoccupied, too prejudiced? Was I attentive? Did I carefully keep my hearing open? How did I regard the creation and creatures of God, especially I who recognize God incarnate in this earth of nations and tribes and tongues and people, in this earth of Christ's brothers? What did I have to see change this year in my most cherished pictures of myself? Did I first let my investments and securities, my politics and my etiquette shape my attitude, and did I then tailor the word of God to meet the details of this prematurely finished portrait? Or did a God whose hour has come finally grasp me with his word?

In the sixteenth century an artist of the Greek Orthodox Church illustrated this scene from the Book of Revelation. He has the angel there, properly fluttering around and precariously suspended in mid air, doing a balancing act with a book. Under him are the people of the world, separated into two clusters. On the one side are the Orthodox Christians; on the other side are the Moslems. All mankind belonged with one or the other. As heirs of the Reformation we have learned to draw another picture. The word of God divides within our heart and bone and marrow, within our Christian community; it cuts through our orthodoxies in the task of causing uproar and change.

Sometimes we think we can have life in the church without suffering, birth without death, resurrection without crucifixion, reformation without a shattering, peace without uproar. Not so, according to the scene of this biblical pageant which we recall and understand only with difficulty and in vagueness. But we who have this scene have not only this from Revelation. We have spoken of the wrong kind of difficulties with this text; there are proper difficulties, too. They center in the fact that Revelation 14 speaks of the word as "an eternal gospel" and we know that gospel is both more and, in part, other than this. The Book of Revelation speaks of "the wrath of the Lamb," but also of the blessedness of those he loves. It speaks of the worthiness of the Creator, but also of his gifts to those who worship the Lamb that was slain. It speaks of repose in the Creator whose word creates uproar in the earth.

The "eternal gospel" is finally phrased in a different way. When we hear it, we have new courage for revival and change. Listen to it as if you never heard it before: God keeps in his heart "plans for welfare and not for evil, to give you a future and a hope" (Jer. 29:11). He does not have "pleasure in the death of the wicked . . . (but) rather that he should turn from his way and live" (Ezek. 18:23). Luther, who spoke of disturbance and uproar as the fate of God's word in the world, also knew it was the word of a God who is "a glowing oven full of love." "As often as God's word is preached, it makes the conscience joyful in the face of God, it enlarges it and gives it certainty. For it is a word of grace, a good and beneficial word."

Because we know that comment, that emphasis about the word from Luther and because we recognize that gospel, we are embarrassed to hear the angel's half of the message. But never forget that the message, while it is partial, is still a message of the word, of the counsel of God whose hour of judgment has come and who calls his creatures to accounting.

No, the most creative thing to do is not to sit on the curb and weep. Rather, having wept, look up and listen: "Fear God and give him glory, for the hour of his judgment has come; and worship him who made heaven and

earth." And look: in the middle of that earth, it is sec-
tioned with a cross. And in the cross is born the church
which still listens to an embarrassing text about an em-
phatic angel. For on that cross and in its darkness we see
that God who has shone in our hearts to give the light of
the knowledge of the glory of God in the face of Christ
(II Cor. 4:6). In that face and in the action of Christ's
life is motive for reviving and change after the uproar
which is the permanent fate of God's word in the world.

FOUR

The Siren Song of Wisdom's Maids

JOHN W. VANNORSDALL

BACCALAUREATE

> *Wisdom has built her house,*
>   *she has set up her seven pillars.*
> *She has slaughtered her beasts,*
>   *she has mixed her wine,*
>   *she has also set her table.*
> *She has sent out her maids to call*
>   *from the highest places in the town,*
> *"Whoever is simple, let him turn in here!"*
>   *To him who is without sense she says,*
> *"Come, eat of my bread*
>   *and drink of the wine I have mixed.*
> *Leave simpleness and live,*
>   *and walk in the way of insight."*
>
>   *—Proverbs 9:1-6*

THESE VERSES FROM THE NINTH chapter of Proverbs present us with a rather seductive image. There is something here for our Admissions Department—a table spread under the trees, maidens in long flowing robes on the top of Huber Hall calling out to all below, "Whoever is simple, let him turn in here." Wine, Women, and Wisdom. The catch is in the brief sentence which follows: "Leave simpleness and live, and walk in the way of insight."

But it is really too late for you now. You listened to the maids, came to the banquet, and now you must pay the price: "Leave simpleness and live, and walk in the way of insight." I suggest what you already know in part: that to walk in the way of insight means to know the complexity of human life; to know the demand for decision which cuts through a simple response to traditional patterns; and to be torn by the disparity between what we know and what we are able to do. In other words, having left simplicity, you must bear the burdens of insight. I should like to indicate in a number of areas what this means to me— and may mean to you.

Call the first area *the problem of living with poverty*. Not your own poverty, of course, for so far as I know, poverty is a vow which none of you have taken; and it takes a vow to be a poverty-stricken American college graduate. All of you will very soon live in at least three rooms, have at least one good suit or dress, more than one pair of shoes, eat some kind of meat at least once a day, have your own transportation, and be protected against sickness and old age. The problem is not your own poverty, but how to enjoy your meat while a man, his wife, and his children stand outside peering through your window, hungry and cold.

This is the risk which you took when you accepted the invitation to walk in the way of insight—the risk of learning that these people are there; the risk of knowing that you are a part of that small number who enjoy the basic necessities of life. You've learned that the haunted faces of the "have nots" reveal a restlessness, that they know of your relative wealth, and that they lay claim to basic necessities as fellow human beings. They will no longer "have not."

You could, perhaps, have rejoiced in simpleness, in the traditional tale that these people are lazy, lacking intelligence, and destined to their lot. Or you might have worn those strange glasses which allow us to see the greater wealth of the man next door but will not let us see the faces pressed against our own window. But Wisdom's maids called from the top of the hill, "Whoever is simple, let him turn in here." And having lost your simpleness, you are now destined to eat your bread in the face of the hungry; destined to be torn by their cry for help and by your own unwillingness and seeming incapacity to do much about it.

A second area is simply *the problem of being human.* Being human involves at least a measure of self-awareness, and a measure of personal freedom in our interaction with the world and in our relationships with one another. The model for this problem is probably our interaction with our parents. Growing self-awareness and self-assertion established the creative tension between our individual needs and desires on the one hand, and parental wisdom and the needs of the family on the other. The way of insight simply extends the breadth with which we understand the problem of the individual as he stands both within and over against the community.

To walk in the way of insight is to acknowledge that

very few of our decisions and actions are without social consequence: that property is never an absolute right; that the bearing of children is not wholly a private matter; that service to our country is never wholly a matter of individual choice; that even the disposal of our remains is rightfully controlled by concern for the welfare of the community.

But the way of insight will also sharpen our awareness of the threat to the range of our freedom. Knowing the demands of mass education, the teacher lives sensitive to the crying needs of individual students. Knowing the needs of the institutional church, the minister lives with the awesome responsibility of individual confrontation. Knowing the military reasons for destroying a village, the soldier must also see the woman with her stick, herding a cow. Knowing the need for a road, the engineer must feel the anguish of an elderly couple watching the destruction of their homestead.

"My God, why can't life be simple?" It will not be. Our numbers grow; the farmer's pasture grows houses with numbers, filled with people who live by the numbers and die by the numbers. And men who polished the hoe with their hands and picked corn with their hands now eat food untouched by human hands from dishes bearing no potter's mark. Some of us will say that we must go back and we'll buy houses with thresholds worn smooth by men of an earlier time, but we know full well that the times will not turn back.

And so we will take profits from stocks in companies we know nothing about, and cast our ballots for men we know nothing about, and drop our fire bombs on villages we know nothing about. But we will not turn our backs on the times because they have brought so much that is good. And perhaps, some day, there will be a way to make us good. The question is, will we still be human?

In simpleness you might not have continued to struggle with the problem of being human—of preserving the self against the community and the community against the self. But the maids were calling, the wine was mixed, and you chose to walk in the way of insight. And now you have no choice but to live in conflict, knowing the value of the machine and not willing to give it up, but knowing also that man needs to leave his fingerprint in the stuff of the world. Knowing the absolute necessity for efficiency in a mass society, you will know also that in the means which efficiency chooses, there is the possibility of removing from man the necessity for moral decision, leaving him stripped of the essence of his humanity.

As for *the problem of living with other races* than our own, it is hard to speak without being trite. Events of the summer, and for some time to come, will take the measure of our prejudice. The time has come when all of us who have sincerely thought that we understood the problem, and honestly wanted to do what is right, will be backed into a corner and beaten with the truth about ourselves.

We may well wish that we could have remained simple, and made the responses of the simple man. For the simple man in the days to come will say, "Integration should move more slowly. The Negro isn't ready. Our schools will suffer. Our property will decrease in value. Our taxes will go up. We will be pushed around."

But you haven't the option of a simple response. Whether you like it or not, you are living during a major social revolution, and you know that revolutions are seldom neat. The stones of a toppled structure fall without discrimination and without begging our pardon. And most of us know, and will know more fully, that the stones need not beg our pardon, for at the very least, we are all guilty of sins of omission.

The white streets of simple men will be dark with anger and sad with whining. But on the street of insight there will be both anguish for personal prejudice discovered and a patient effort to rebuild the structures of our society, this time in color.

"Come," say the maids, "eat of my bread and drink of the wine I have mixed." And you've come to Wisdom's banquet and now you must pay the price—"Leave simpleness and live, and walk in the way of insight."

This is the burden of the educated man in three of a dozen areas: to have much bread, but to eat in the face of poverty's children, acknowledging our unwillingness and incapacity to do much about it, to know both the need of the community for our conformity and our need as human beings to stand over and against the community, asserting our right as individuals to make moral judgments; to face a social revolution without the excuses of a simple man, with enough insight to know that we are called to a creative rebuilding of the social structure and cannot avoid personal anguish.

Since I am a chaplain it would be logical for you to expect now some religious oil for all these troubled waters. I conclude with two simple things, and you may judge for yourselves how much is oil for troubled waters and how much is salt for open wounds.

The first is this: that to whatever extent we turn to the God of the Old and New Testaments, just to that extent will our conflicts and tensions be increased. To allow God to impinge upon our lives is to open ourselves to an increasingly painful understanding of the despair of hungry and homeless men. It is as though wherever God is, there are they. Whenever he speaks, we hear their voice. And the words that are spoken are always an indictment of our best intentions.

To allow God to impinge upon our dilemma of the community on the one hand and the individual on the other is to hear a radical judgment upon competing idols, both of our own creation, both of which become demonic and destructive of human freedom. Many of us would testify that the problem of being human is not ultimately to be answered by pitting the individual against the community or the community against the individual, but that our life as individuals in the community will be rightly ordered and truly free only when submitted to the will and mercy of God himself.

To allow the suffering God of Jesus Christ to probe the depth of our prejudice is more painful a prospect than most of us have been able to allow. It is not safe to expect that God will minimize the conflicts and tensions which we face. The whole record of his activity in history has been a record of men driven to face their compromises and forced to live at the edge of life where truth is harsh and the conflicts sharp and where the really important decisions are being made.

If there is any comfort, it lies in this: it is precisely out here, at the edge of life, in the midst of the conflict, that God is known, where he is at work, where he bestows his greatest gifts and grants his strange kind of peace.

It is when a man is increasingly exposed to the disparity

of his wealth and the world's poverty—half mad with the divine command that he do what he cannot, or does not, do —it is here that the mercy of God means freedom and life, and a new beginning.

It is when a man is suffocating in the demonic arms of a mass society that he learns to rejoice in the God who himself suffers man's tragic alienation rather than force man into the mold of compliance to make him good.

It is when a man is beaten with the truth of his own prejudice and comes to know the lie of all his easy speeches —it is then that such a man might come to rejoice even in the strange and terrible forgiveness of God which sets him free of the past to share the building of the future.

This is the place where the Spirit of God moves to call these people, to enlighten and sanctify.

The siren song of Wisdom's maids has brought you to the way of insight. The consequence, to one degree or another, is that you will live in the midst of conflict and tension. But it is here also where you may find the strange peace of God.

FIVE

Letter Home

JOHN W. VANNORSDALL

A SERVICE FOR THE PARENTS OF UNDERGRADUATES

I asked the student committee for this morning to make suggestions for this sermon. The suggestion was logical, I guess: that I say something about mothers. This is a hard thing to do, and I have chosen to come at it in the form of a letter. A letter long overdue.

DEAR MOTHER AND DAD:

THERE WERE MANY THINGS WHICH I wanted to say to you while I was home for Easter, and I just didn't get around to it . . . just as I didn't get around to it after exams, or at Christmas time, or last summer; and probably won't this summer. It's not really that there isn't time. It's just that I can't be sure the words will be right . . . that I can say what I'm thinking so you'll understand.

You both know that my feeling for you runs deep. Fathers and sons say this in a handshake. Mothers need some words, too, and it's the words that are hard.

Maybe daughters have some feeling about this business of being carried and born and nursed. I hope you won't

47

take offense when I say that a son going on twenty-one is a little negative about those bear-rug pictures. Rationally, we know that we have this biological origin and tie, but we try so hard to be independent and adult that it's hard to admit such a puny beginning. Maybe daughters feel the same way. I don't know.

There is another way in which I've come to understand our relationship with one another. This will sound sort of academic and stiff. I don't really understand it yet . . . maybe I never will. I mean that psychologists tell us that even before we are born, and in the earliest years, our parents give a shape to our humanness—to what we will be like as people. Not just inherited traits, but our sense of security . . . our attitudes toward life and other people and situations we must face. The way in which you felt about me as an infant, the way in which you cared for me, comforted me, disciplined me—the way in which you did things for me, and made me do things for myself—the way in which the two of you related to each other—all these things were important in shaping me as a social being, as a person.

And this is the growing edge of my gratitude toward you. Every warm holding, every gift of food, every interesting sound, every calling of me by name, every marking of my separate identity, every discipline which told me that what I did was important to you—these were the marks of love and caring which nurtured my humanity. My debt to you is nothing less than my humanness. How can I say "thanks" for that? But I want to.

Mother will worry some about this, because she'll wonder about the things not done—the times of anger or despair, or too much or too little discipline . . . and how

48

much it may have affected me . . . or changed what might have been. Forget it! No, that's too flip. But isn't this the relevance of our religion? To do the best we can, and know full well that it is neither enough, nor perfect, and know that we have a gracious and forgiving God who really expects us to rejoice even in the face of our imperfectness, both yours and mine?

Strange, isn't it, that in going away to college I have in fact begun to discover the deep bonds which will always bind us. Not so much the genes which determine the color of my skin, eyes, and hair, or my features—but what you are as persons, and to one another; your capacity to hold me close and set me free—to pick me up with compassion, and to show me your displeasure. In this deep, deep way, I am your child . . . and deeply grateful.

I'm also becoming aware of some of the costs of having children. Not just in money; that's obvious enough. But the personal cost of loving a child.

I was thinking the other day about my first two-wheeled bicycle, purchased mostly with your money, but some with mine. Enough with my money, at least, so that I could feel that it was my bicycle. And this was a kind of turning point in our relationship. I was no longer totally dependent upon the two of you for my humanness, for my existence. Enough on my own to have a bicycle to travel farther from home—taking part of my security from having learned to ride it—part of my sense of personal importance now taken from the kids my own age—being nurtured by some of my teachers, who also saw some worth in me.

So I'm beginning to understand that the love of a parent causes suffering in the very fulfillment of its purpose. You love me into an increasingly independent and separate human being . . . and as I become just that, I begin to take my life from other relationships. The response which I make is not to you alone, but to others who now receive more and more of my time, my admiration and affection.

This was so clear when I started going with Jane. Because you love me, you want to love Jane too. But I can see the struggle that it involves. She now shares the deep things which long ago I shared with you. It's just a fact that when I come home now, it's to see you, of course, but Jane takes most of my time, which you know, and my thought, which you surely sense. Hard as it is for you . . . you complain so little and seem to understand. And I'm grateful for that . . . that your love can be great enough to let me go. The amazing thing is that the more I understand of how hard it is to love a child into independence, the deeper my respect and love for you. This must be the meaning of the Bible when it says that it's what we give away that we receive again—that it's in the giving of our life, not in the grasping of it, that our life is given to us.

There's a final thing, and it's not resolved in my mind . . . but I share it with you. It has to do with what I do with my life. You remember my telling you about Salinger's *Catcher in the Rye*. I really had the feel of that . . . that a lot of life is phony, and that it would be somehow authentic to be the catcher in the rye, who keeps the children from falling over the cliff.

Well, it turns out to be more complicated than that . . . as I guess you knew. It turns out that sometimes the catcher in the rye has to go down the cliff to rescue some of the kids, and sometimes he falls. It's like the good shepherd in the Bible, which I always thought was quite a nice idea. Then I found out that it was this same good shepherd who died on Good Friday. Somehow it seemed as though they were two different people, and I could have one without the other.

I've been reading some of the old documents in English constitutional history, the root of so much of our liberty today. For example, an interesting thing happened on December 8, 1534. A man named Ralph Broke went out to look at a common pasture. Some enemies of his started to beat him up. A friend of Ralph's ran to the village and raised a hue and cry. Thomas and John Dassheffen and Nicholas Mosely ran out into the country and saved him from being killed. The thing is, they took a bit of a beating, too, and later had to appear in court in what turned out to be a very nasty business.

Let me tell you too about Peter de la Mare. Back in 1376, almost six hundred years ago, the King of England called a parliament. The nobles told the commoners, who included some knights, that they should meet separately. So first the commons decided that they should try as honestly as they could to figure out what needed to be done in order to make England a better place to live. And after three days, they were ready to report to the King and his counsellors. And they chose Peter to speak for them. The report of his response is amazing. "And the said Peter, out of reverence to God and his good companions, and for the benefit of the kingdom, assumed that duty." [1]

Now what I'm trying to say is this: you taught me to believe that there are times when, out of reverence for God and for the good of the nation . . . I should assume my duty. And there are many times in today's world when I

[1] Carl Stephenson and Frederick Marcham, *Sources of English Constitutional History.* (New York: Harper and Brothers, 1937.) p. 222.

would give anything to be Peter de la Mare, and represent the commons before the nobles and speak for the good of the realm. I think you would want me to do it, too. But I also get the feeling within myself, and from you, and from my friends—that this could result in a lot of grief, that those who respond to the hue and the cry end up beaten and in court. I suppose every mother would like her son to be Paul Revere—but I wonder how many would hand him a musket, and tell him to get out there and die.

You have your dreams for me, and I for myself. But there's a conflict in the dreams. Safety and the good things of life don't always go hand in hand with doing my duty out of reverence for God and for the good of the realm.

Stay with me on this one, will you? When in small ways, I am chosen to speak for the commons, support me in that —because I've learned it from you. When I choose to stay indoors, and close my ears to the hue and cry—I guess I learned something of that from you, too.

It's a funny thing about this good shepherd. I used to think that all the sheep were either black or white—either good little sheep, or gone astray. It turns out that all are a lighter or a darker gray. The amazing thing is that the good shepherd doesn't equivocate because of this—affirming me, in spite of my shortcomings toward you and my neighbor—affirming you, in spite of whatever shortcomings you may have—sustaining our common life, enriching us through one another . . . all at great cost to himself, just as your love for me has been at great cost—a cost which I hope that I can pay as well.

With thanksgiving to God for this and for all growth in understanding between us, I remain

Your grateful son.

SIX

The Office of Shepherd Today

ANDREW J. WHITE, III

NOTE: The demand for equal rights for all citizens of the United States has produced turmoil and confusion in community after community. In Cleveland, Ohio not long ago the board of education was accused of segregationist motivation in relation to its school building program. Massive protest was raised by the proponents of civil rights, some groups even attempting to block the construction of certain new buildings. On April 7, 1964 a young Presbyterian clergyman, Bruce Klunder, was crushed by a bulldozer in such a demonstration. Many persons in Cleveland publicly called his death a foolish waste. In response to this tragic event, the following sermon was delivered.

"I am the good shepherd. The good shepherd lays down his life for the sheep. He who is a hireling and not a shepherd, whose own the sheep are not, sees the wolf coming and leaves the sheep and flees; and the wolf snatches them and scatters them. He flees because he is a hireling and cares nothing for the sheep. I am the good shepherd; I know my own and my own know me, as the Father knows me and I know the Father; and I lay down my life for the sheep. And I have other sheep, that are not of this fold; I

must bring them also, and they will heed my voice. So there shall be one flock, one shepherd."

—*John 10:11-16*

... Christ also suffered for you, leaving you an example, that you should follow in his steps.

—*1 Peter 2:21*

I AM NOT A MYSTIC BUT I CALL to your attention something which hit me hard on the afternoon of Tuesday, April 7, in Cleveland, Ohio. It was nothing more than the simple fact that I do not pick the lessons that are read on a Sunday morning. You are aware of the fact that our church has followed the practice of using pericopes chosen centuries ago. It happens that on this particular Sunday the appointed Gospel says: "I am the good shepherd, the good shepherd lays down his life for the sheep." There *must* be something in the word of God that is coming forth.

And the appointed Epistle says: "Christ also suffered for you leaving you an example that you should follow in his steps . . ." There *must* be some sort of meaning here.

Now look back at the good shepherd, Jesus Christ. Don't you suppose there are some people who, after it was over, said that he was young and foolish, and that it was all a waste. I suppose there were a good many who said, "He could have done so much more if he had just stayed alive —the fool!" You know, he didn't have to go to the cross. Have you thought about that this week? Why Jesus Christ went to the cross? He did not go to incite a mob, but he went to the cross because he was obedient, that's all. He went to the cross because he felt it was his father's will and

54

he prayed, "Thy will be done." No one, in the family of faith at least, accuses Jesus Christ of committing suicide; we rather glorify him as St. Paul did, for he "became obedient even unto death" (Phil. 2:8). I charge you to think clearly of the difference between obedience and suicide.

Think back to the church itself as it spans the centuries. Clearly, the church has been called to be the suffering servant of Jesus Christ. This is why in hymnody, in Christian tradition, in Christian literature, the martyrs are praised because they became suffering servants. They show forth the church as it follows Jesus Christ in obedience—for those who follow Jesus are faithful in their obedience. There are even some who believe that the crucifixion of Jesus Christ has been and will be reenacted in various ways by various people and that perhaps an obedient Christian will prove from time to time to be a very clear reminder of what the good shepherd did.

Now, I ask you, who can understand what the good shepherd did? Believing man can hardly understand the cross of Jesus Christ and non-believing man cannot comprehend it at all. Those whose lives are ruled solely by self-interest cannot comprehend why Jesus Christ died on a cross. It is folly for the Greeks, remember? It looks like sheer stupidity to the Jews. Only to the man of spirit, only to the man of faith does the cross of Jesus Christ become even slightly comprehensible. But at least we in the church try to understand why he went to his death when he could have prevented it. We try to understand the Christ.

Now let's turn to the events of this past week. It seems to me that we of the church owe it to society to try to be the interpreters of something which is incomprehensible,

55

for as far as I know, we are the only ones who have even a slight comprehension of the obedience which was demonstrated by Jesus. How can we expect the myriads of unbelieving men to understand? How can we expect those who are guided only by self-interest to understand? The proclamation which needs to be made is that of the cross. Only in the light of the cross can we understand the events of this past week—and, let me warn you, only in the light of the cross will we be able to understand the events of the weeks that are to come.

Now let it be said loud and let it be clear and let there be no mistake: Bruce Klunder did not want to die. I say this as a friend of Bruce Klunder who had breakfast with him on the morning he died; I say this as one who was in the group who argued with Bruce Klunder about the method which he finally used to show his protest; and I say this as one who disagreed with him. But he was one who did not want to die. Let us be interpreters of that fact. Also, let us be interpreters of the fact that he did die because he was obedient.

We should be able to understand this. We've had missionary heroes, and they have done some silly things. We have known persons who risked and even lost their lives on faraway shores because they felt that the gospel of Jesus Christ needed to be proclaimed. We've known of the martyrs who died for their faith. We have seen outsiders with nothing personal to gain who nevertheless have felt so firmly that justice needed to be done that they have been obedient and have come within this line. Within the church we know that for the will of the Lord, men have always died; because they have felt in harmony with the will of God, men have died rather than compromise.

The issues in this Cleveland mess center around things which you don't read in the newspapers. Are men under God equal? That's the chief issue. Do men under God who are equal then have equal opportunity to learn and equal opportunity to achieve? There's a difference, you know. A lot of people blame the minority for not achieving anything when they know full well, though they refuse to admit it, that they've never given the minority an opportunity to learn. How can you achieve without free opportunity? Are some prevented from equality? These are the issues.

It's not necessary to go into a long list of how people are prevented. They are prevented—sometimes by outward direct action, sometimes by subtle indirect action, sometimes by inaction. Nor is this the time or the place to raise questions about strategy. There is a time, there is a place for these questions. By these questions many people have tried to sidetrack themselves and others from the sheer reality of our brothers' suffering, from the subtle indignities which we foster, from the guilt which society bears. The real question which Christians must be asking themselves, though, is what must we do to be obedient as the suffering servant church of Jesus Christ! One never gets to that question if he takes all of his energy to criticize the method or the way some other has chosen to follow. It seems to me that this is the time for introspection. I wish we could have had a moratorium for introspection, but people seem to choose to fight about minor side issues instead of coming to grips with their own responsibility.

I ask you to look at the alternatives. In our metropolitan area there are, at the present time, two examples of the same general question. Perhaps you have not realized that this whole issue surrounding the schools and the methods being used to protest the school building program is exactly the same question which surrounds the freeway controversy in Shaker Heights.

The only difference between these two controversies, as I see it, is the alternatives available to the participants. The claim is registered against the Negroes in the ghetto that they are not properly constituted to register a protest. The issue is not the merits of their protest, but rather the question, do they have a right to be heard? The school board says, "No, they do not." Do the residents of Shaker Heights—with their citizens' freeway committee—have *more* right to register their protest against the freeway's path with the legally constituted authorities who plan and execute freeways in our society?

The alternatives which the protesting groups have are quite different. Shaker Heights, where education and opportunity are real, Shaker Heights, where wealth is a fact of life, has many alternatives. Protestors there are able by virtue of their wealth to produce a great deal of literature. In the last two months they have been able to see to it that almost daily before their crisis time came, you read something in the newspaper of their activity. They have been able, as one man told me in this past week, to bring certain economic pressures to bear upon the governor of the state who knows he needs a few votes in Shaker Heights. Their next battle line is to have the governor intercede, and you watch, he will.

A similar grass roots operation, coming out of the Hazeldell Parents Association and the United Freedom Movement, comprised mainly of Negro people, does not have the same alternatives of action. Newspapers are inclined to equate them with persons who are not responsible. There is a wide difference. I was there Tuesday afternoon. I saw it. Don't let anybody tell you that the demonstrators were a mob. They were not. I saw a mob develop after Bruce's death, but no demonstrators were in it. The mob needs to be controlled, but how can a mob be controlled if the responsible people will not talk to one another?

The alternatives in the ghetto are limited. There is no wealth to produce literature. There has not been equal opportunity to learn and therefore there has not been equal opportunity to achieve. What does such a group do when those who are in office officially refuse to talk? What would you do? Perhaps you would not lie down behind the bulldozer. Would you walk out into the street merely to show your neighbors and your friends that you feel you have something on your side going for you? Would you do that? I grant you that if I start walking around this church with a sign to protest your treatment of me, I may contribute to some violent feelings within you. But, on the other hand, if you walk by me—being able to do something, like talking to me to help me understand or removing my grievances— but you refuse to talk with me, have you not also contributed to some violent feelings? Perhaps within someone who had been simply watching us both across the street. Don't place the guilt at any single source.

In a democracy do we not have the right to talk over differences? But if you are prevented from talking then what do you do? I wish I had the answer.

When I look back through history I see the shameful but true fact that often extreme measures which we may not like have been necessary to wake up the majority to its tyranny over a minority. Now, it seems to me, it's altogether too easy for us to absolve ourselves from guilt by belittling the sacrifice of a Christian who is obedient. I think that the death of my friend Bruce Klunder ought to drive me to my knees for—even as Christ was crucified not by one or two but by us all, so insofar as we sit comfortably, quietly, unwilling to be the suffering servant church—*we* have no reason to absolve ourselves from his death.

Eugene Carson Blake, the stated clerk of the General Assembly of the Presbyterian Church, here for Bruce's funeral, said that our need is for more exposure to one another. I admit that for me personally it has made a great deal of difference in my feelings on some of these issues to know at first hand the subtly direct or indirect inhumanity of man to man. Four years ago I arranged to be the roommate of Pastor Allen Youngblood at one of our conference meetings in Stuebenville. Because he was a Negro, we were forced to drive ten miles outside Steubenville to find a motel that would house us. I admit that this makes a little difference in how I feel on the issue. One of my parishioners came to me when he was kept from a promotion in his job because of his race. It would have been a logical promotion adhering to all the rules of seniority. I admit that this makes a difference in how I feel on the issue.

When I see the products of ghetto schools, I know that this is not simply a matter of race but of the deprivation of opportunity, that is, the majority depriving the ghetto child, white and Negro alike, of the best possible learning opportunity. The ghetto schools just don't measure up in this town. You know full well you'd rather have your kids going to East Cleveland or Cleveland Heights schools than to Cleveland schools, especially east side Cleveland schools. Now you can blame that on the Negro if you want to, but it seems far more logical to me to blame it on the fact of the white vacuum, an absence of leadership that has just left and/or has refused to give opportunity.

I admit it affects me when I see people who are unable to achieve simply because they have been prevented from opportunity. There are some people who don't achieve because they are lazy. Sometimes my wife says I'm lazy and I suspect you've heard that too. But when I see people prevented from achieving because they are not allowed the opportunity, this makes a difference. Whenever one of my friends is unable to buy a house because the banks and the real estate people say "Oh no, in this area on the map, right here only, you can live"—in the last four or five years I have gotten to know some people who have had this experience—I admit that this too makes a difference.

Well, it's been quite a week. My hope is, my prayer is, that it has helped others see the urgency of the call to equality. I don't see how our society can exist if we tolerate inequality. And by the way, once we solve this race problem, let me warn you that this thing of poverty and unemployment is really going to be a problem. I don't care whether you're white or Negro, it's getting to be a sin to be poor in our society and that's a real issue.

Let me say something to you with all the love in a pastor's heart, but in terms of my responsibility to declare a spade a spade or a sin a sin—and it's this: to the degree that you still have some confusion in your mind or some hesitancy or question about the basic right of men to equality of opportunity to achieve, to the degree that you have this questioning, you deny the influence of the Christ. I charge you to come to grips with it. You must live with your conscience. For I point out to you again, non-believing man has never been able to comprehend the death of Jesus Christ. The task of the church is to try to break through, to understand how the Christ could have been so "stupid" as to allow himself to be obedient unto death.

The church is the church of the shepherd who in obedience died. In the Epistle for today it says, "Christ also suffered for you, leaving you an example, that you should follow in his steps." Does this not also mean that we are called upon to suffer? Doesn't it mean that we are to bear the cross? I charge you to think and to interpret the cross of Jesus Christ. It won't be easy.

The "Private" World

of Life and Death

SEVEN

Happiness or the Hand of God?

H. GEORGE ANDERSON

"A little while, and you will see me no more; again a little while, and you will see me." Some of his disciples said to one another, "What is this that he says to us, 'A little while, and you will not see me, and again a little while, and you will see me'; and, 'because I go to the Father'?" They said, "What does he mean by 'a little while'? We do not know what he means." Jesus knew that they wanted to ask him; so he said to them, "Is this what you are asking yourselves, what I meant by saying, 'A little while, and you will not see me, and again a little while, and you will see me'? Truly, truly, I say to you, you will weep and lament, but the world will rejoice; you will be sorrowful, but your sorrow will turn into joy. When a woman is in travail she has sorrow, because her hour has come; but when she is delivered of the child, she no longer remembers the anguish, for joy that a child is born into the world. So you have sorrow now, but I will see you again and your hearts will rejoice, and no one will take your joy from you."

—John 16:16-22

THIS IS THE SUNDAY CALLED "Jubilate," because the first words of the Introit for today are "Make a joyful noise unto the Lord." An old pastor once told me that this verse from Psalm 100 was his favorite, because he never could sing very well, and he was glad that David had recognized that those who couldn't sing could at least "make a joyful noise." So this Sunday is for everyone—everyone is included in the cry, "Make a joyful noise unto the Lord."

If there is any command in the whole of scripture that we Americans should find easy, it should be this: to be joyful. Or, as Paul says to the Thessalonians, "Rejoice always" (I Thess. 5:16). We have less to worry about, more to enjoy, and more time for enjoyment than most nations have had before. In fact, the pursuit of happiness is written into the Declaration of Independence as one of our inalienable rights. Why do we have to be reminded, then, to rejoice? Doesn't that just come naturally?

Yes, it does, but we must be careful about our words here, because "happiness" in the usual sense is not what the Bible means when it talks about "joy" and "rejoicing." The sculptor Rodin has made this very clear in two small statues which he called "The Hand of the Devil" and "The Hand of God." One of these is of smoothly polished marble and shows a cupped hand cradling a human figure. Everything is peaceful, and the figure lies there limp, inert, untroubled. It is something of a shock to see that the sculptor has carved on *this* statue, "The Hand of the Devil." His meaning is clear, though, when we turn to his symbol for "The Hand of God." Here much of the stone is quarry-rough, but thrusting upward from its center is a powerful hand which seems to cleave the marble with its motion. In its grip this hand also has a human figure, carrying it upward out of unconsciousness into life.

It's so easy to mistake the hand of the Devil for the hand of God—so easy to seek static happiness instead of dynamic joy. For that's just what these two words represent.

Think for a moment about your own private idea of happiness. You probably have a picture in your mind right now about what it would be like. Do you see yourself at a large desk with "President" on a brass plaque? Or do you see a new house with your name on the mailbox? Maybe you see a fireplace with happy grandchildren romping on the floor—or perhaps right now you smile with inner satisfaction as you think of this afternoon, the paper in your lap, a ball game on TV, the children playing outside, and yourself cradled in the well-upholstered arms of a lounging chair. That's happiness. That's what the Declaration of Independence guarantees you.

Or is it? Remember what those wise old founding fathers said? They never hoped to guarantee happiness—only the *pursuit* of happiness, and that's a far, far different thing. It is not the happiness that is inevitable, but only the constant struggle to reach it. Doesn't that bring to mind the disturbing picture of the carrot and the horse—that carrot that always dangles before his nose, always just one step away, one more step away? *That's* the pursuit of happiness. That's what life guarantees you—not the happiness, but the pulling, and the struggling, and the straining, and the final, inevitable disappointment. It reminds me of those fairy stories that used to enchant me. Remember how so many of them had three wishes? Three wishes to get all your heart desired—three wishes to bring perfect happiness. But there was wisdom in those ancient tales, for the three wishes were never enough. They never brought happiness, but always disappointment.

And so it is with those pictures you carry in your heart. Behind that desk with the "President" sign sits a troubled man, not a happy man. You think, "On that salary I wouldn't mind being a little troubled," but you surely have lived long enough to know that previous raises have not brought the kind of happiness you want. In fact, you were probably just about as happy ten years ago, when your salary was considerably less than it is right now. Or that home in the suburbs with your name on the mailbox. Maybe you have it already, but there may be a mortgage, need for an extra bedroom, or difficult neighbors. Real happiness still lies ahead—like the carrot. Even the simple happiness of a drowsy Sunday afternoon may prove hard to find, for as you lie there in that TV chair your mind is plagued by half-a-dozen other things you *should* be doing. And so it is with happiness—like a desert mirage, it is always "just ahead."

When the Bible speaks about "joy," however, it means something quite different. Joy is like "The Hand of God" sculpture, thrusting upward out of difficulty. Joy has the note of victory over hardship, of conquest over defeat. Notice how often the Bible stresses this contrast. "Weeping may tarry for the night, but joy comes with the morning" (Psalm 30:5). In Jeremiah we read that mourning is turned to joy before God (31:13). This theme of victory swells to a mighty chorus in the New Testament. When the woman found her lost coin and the shepherd his lost sheep, they cried to their neighbors, "Rejoice with me," for the lost had been found (Luke 15:9). James urges us to "count it all joy when you meet various trials" (1:2), and the book of Hebrews reminds us that Christ himself, because of the joy set before him, endured the cross, despising the shame (12:2). In the Gospel for today Christ told his disciples "you will be sorrowful, but your sorrow will be turned into joy."

These Bible passages only serve to underline something we already know, but tend to forget. What we call the "joyous" moments in life are really the moments of victory over some difficulty. The first time a child stands alone, or the first carefully formed syllable of speech; the joy of graduation day, with the long months of study behind; the joy of promotion or advancement in business—all of these moments share one common basis: accomplishment. By effort a victory has been won. That's joy, and often its sign is not easy laughter, but tears.

The best part of it is that joy is possible for everyone. No one can be completely happy, but everyone can know the thrill of these moments of joy.

Now there's a snake in every garden—even the Garden of Eden had one. And the trouble with joy is that it doesn't last. To most people it comes in moments—short periods of gaiety with long stretches of dry, everyday living in between. Like oases in the desert, these moments of joy are few.

These little victories we win are only partial victories in a life-long battle. In the War of 1812 the British won every army battle they fought, and yet they lost the war. That's the way it is with us. Take for example those moments of joy mentioned a while ago. It is wonderful when a child first takes a step or stands alone, but these accomplishments are soon forgotten in the struggle to learn new words or the complicated process of climbing. When those are mastered, then comes reading, writing, and reckoning. Or graduation. I felt like the king of the world when I graduated from high school, but just three months later I was the lowest of the low, a college freshman. And this process is most clear in our life's work, because here we run up against the plain fact that our accomplishments don't go on forever. There is an end. We can climb so high on life's ladder, but we always race against time. I know a man who built up a fine business all by himself; but he is over sixty now, and no matter how successful the next years are for him, deep inside there is the question, "How much good is it?" He has no son to follow in his steps, no assurance that what he has carefully built up will not disintegrate when he is gone. He doesn't want to take it with him; he just longs to know that the business will continue. Yet this assurance he cannot have. Joys are like cut flowers; they may last for longer or shorter periods, but eventually, they will fade for time is their enemy. "Time like an everrolling stream bears all its sons away," and that same irresistible tide carries our joys away too.

But the Christian lives in a different dimension. He has a joy that is complete, a joy that never fades because time cannot touch it. Other joys fail because they are partial; Christ told his disciples that their joy would be "full," complete. "So you have sorrow now, but I will see you again and your hearts will rejoice, and no one will take your joy from you." Only to the Christian comes neverending joy.

When we hear the words, "But I will see you again and your hearts will rejoice," we tend to think of the last day, of the coming of Christ in glory—but that is not what Jesus meant. These words and this promise are recorded in the sixteenth chapter of St. John's Gospel, when Christ was warning his disciples about his coming passion. When he says to them "you will weep and lament, but the world will rejoice," he was thinking of the crucifixion which lay just ahead. And when he said "you will be sorrowful, but your sorrow will be turned to joy," he was thinking of his resurrection appearances. In other words, the joy that no one could take away is the result of the resurrection. It is a joy connected with the final victory—the triumph over death. This is the victory of Easter.

Even though we still live in a world of change, where children grow up and move away, where houses deteriorate and jobs become stale, we are lifted by God's hand to see beyond the confusion. To paraphrase the Old Testament lesson for today (Isaiah 40:25-31): when we are "down in the dumps," God can lift us and give our hearts wings; when we have been running from one thing to another until we "run down," God will bring us out of weariness; when we must walk those long dull stretches of everyday life, God's hand will support our fainting spirits. This fact is not changed by the passage of time, by the aging of our bodies, or by death itself. Like a great rock jutting above the stream of time, this hope remains immovable and undeniable. In all the changes and partial hopes of this life there is one relationship that cannot weaken or grow old, because it is with a living God. ". . . neither death, nor life, nor angels, nor principalities, nor things present, nor things to come, nor powers, nor height, nor depth, nor anything else in all creation, will be able to separate us from the love of God in Christ Jesus our Lord (Romans 8:38-39). This is our confidence, and this joy no one can take from us.

EIGHT

In Defense of Materialism

PAUL F. BOSCH

On the third day there was a marriage at Cana in Galilee, and the mother of Jesus was there; Jesus also was invited to the marriage, with his disciples. When the wine failed, the mother of Jesus said to him, "They have no wine." And Jesus said to her, "O woman, what have you to do with me? My hour has not yet come." His mother said to the servants, "Do whatever he tells you." Now six stone jars were standing there, for the Jewish rites of purification, each holding twenty or thirty gallons. Jesus said to them, "Fill the jars with water." And they filled them up to the brim. He said to them, "Now draw some out, and take it to the steward of the feast." So they took it. When the steward of the feast tasted the water now become wine, and did not know where it came from (though the servants who had drawn the water knew), the steward of the feast called the bridegroom and said to him, "Every man serves the good wine first; and when men have drunk freely, then the poor wine; but you have kept the good wine until now." This, the first of his signs, Jesus did at Cana in Galilee, and manifested his glory; and his disciples believed in him.

—John 2:1-11

IT HAPPENS AT OUR HOME THAT, in accordance with our usual time schedule, there are as of this moment, by actual count, no less than seventeen Christmas gifts still to be delivered. I don't think there are any more than that. Now I have been pondering the theological implications of this oppressive domestic reality, and I have considered preaching a sermon this morning with the title, "How to Give a Christmas Gift Four Weeks Late Without Embarrassment." You'll be glad to know that I gave up that idea, and decided instead to speak in defense of materialism. But actually the first title could still obtain, because I want to say something too about the giving of gifts. I choose as text the record of the wedding party in John 2, partly for sentimental reason, and partly because it applies.

I believe you must begin with a love, a respect for the things of this world. You will also end here, incidentally, but this is the beginning place too. You simply cannot become a good materialist unless you start off with the right presuppositions. And this is one of them: that the things of this material world are good in their own right.

I stress this because so often we begin with just the opposite attitude. We begin with the assumption that things —the material, the physical, all that goes with it—aren't good, but bad. We've somewhere got the notion, I suppose from Greek philosophy by way of countless pious Christian teachers and preachers, that what the Christian faith is really concerned with—what God is really concerned with —is not, after all, the material side of life, but the immaterial, not the physical things, but rather, the spiritual values. And the implication is that Christian people ought to have the same standards. Our concern ought not to be with the body but with the soul, not the finite but the infinite, not the mortal but the immortal, not the mutable but the immutable, not the contingencies of historical existence but the certainties of eternal truths. We ought not to worry about things. We ought to concern ourselves with ideas . . . and so on.

Now this viewpoint certainly has a popular following, especially among people you'd normally label as religious. This is what religion for many is supposed to be all about, an affirmation of eternal certainties, changeless truths, immutable ideas, in the face of and in opposition to the vagaries of history, the contingencies of existence. To many, this is exactly what religion is supposed to teach, this is exactly what religionists are supposed to believe.

Now although this viewpoint is certainly popular, it represents a direct contradiction to the actual life of perhaps ninety-nine per cent of the population of this campus. I mean those in the arts and those in the sciences. Most of you, ninety-nine per cent of you, can call yourselves either artists or scientists. And it would seem to me that you can't spiritualize either the artist or his art, the scientist or his science, without doing grave harm all around. Physics, chemistry, biology, engineering: these sciences deal with things, real palpable things, and the scientist is living out a terrible contradiction if he lives and works six days each week with things, with the physical, material world, and yet feels called upon to believe on Sundays that things aren't important, or that they're somehow base and not worth the concern of the religious man. And the artist is living out a terrible contradiction too, if he lives and works with canvas and brush, or stone and steel for six days and on Sunday feels he must deny their worth, their importance, because after all the best things in life are "spiritual," and after all, God isn't interested in canvas, sculpture, or architecture.

Now it may come as a comfort to you if you are that kind of a scientist or that kind of an artist, that the overwhelming witness of the Bible testifies to exactly the opposite viewpoint. The overwhelming witness of the Bible is actually a kind of materialism that asserts the goodness of creation, that things as well as ideas are dear to God—things like atoms, molecules, rocks, trees, chairs, buildings, organs, tissues, muscles, as well as philosophical speculation, or abstract thought, or spiritual values. Every part of God's creation is potentially an instrument in God's service, and historic Christian teaching has never recognized a distinction between material and immaterial, physical and spiritual. Historic Christian teaching has rather recognized another distinction, quite different, emancipating to me in its difference. Dr. Gabriel Vahanian has reminded us of this historic biblical position in his book, *The Death of God*[1] where he cites Martin Buber. He says the Christian recognizes only two categories of things in this world: the holy, and the not yet holy. And although Christian materialism must end here, with this assertion, it must also begin here. The things of this world are either holy, or they are not yet holy but will one day be holy, that is, consecrated, set aside for divine purposes.

That's first and probably most important: we are to love and respect, I would even say reverence, the things of this world because they are potentially holy things. I read this affirmation throughout the Bible. I read it also in the story of the wedding party where Christ exhibits this love, this

[1] Gabriel Vahanian, *The Death of God* (New York: Braziller, 1961).

reverence towards water and towards wine. Our Christian materialism is to be of this kind, one that indiscriminately loves and cherishes and reverences all the things of creation as either holy or potentially holy. I have a great sympathy and fondness for the current movement in sculpture known as the art of assemblage, or *merzbild*. Junk pictures is what they are, sculptures sometimes of great humor or beauty or sensitivity, made entirely of cast-off junk. Here is simply another reminder that nothing in this world is too dirty, too common, too humble, too "physical," too "secular" to participate in these, the only two categories the Christian admits: the holy, the not yet holy.

Now that's first. And this is second: these humble, common things, loved and respected and reverenced in their own right, are to be taken up, to be offered by the hands of love.

So, for instance, with the wine at the wedding party. It may be either holy or not yet holy, perhaps depending on in whose hands it is offered, in whose hands it is taken. Here it is taken up in the hands of love, the hands of Jesus, his mother, his disciples.

Now there's a warning implicit here, is there not? It's the warning against a wrong use of the things of creation. God's creation is good; all the things of his creation are good things: that's part of our Christian materialism. And this is another part: the warning that this goodness can be corrupted. So it is with every good gift. There is always the possibility of perversion, and "the whole creation has been groaning in travail . . ." (Romans 8:22).

I believe that there are several temptations always present when a man as scientist or as artist begins to take this kind of materialism seriously. And you don't have to be just a scientist or artist in the strictest sense to take this seriously—I'm suggesting and commending this materialism to you, wherever you are. There are several temptations here, and the chief temptation is idolatry.

We have a record of the course of this idolatry in Genesis II, where in mythological and poetic language we are told of the building of the Tower of Babel. Here is an example of materialism gotten out of hand, idolatrous passions worshipping the gift rather than the giver, loving the creation rather than the creator, putting trust in stone and brick and art and technology, and not in the Lord of heaven and earth. Now that's idolatry, and you remember the result: a glorious work never completed, brought to ruin, and even more pitiably, human communion, human community, shattered in a confusion of tongues. The great and thrilling promise of art—that here is a kind of language that all men may understand, a language universal even beyond the language of words—is thus thwarted, subverted; men live instead in hopeless confusion. And the great and thrilling promise of science and technology—that here too is a kind of language that all men may understand, another language universal beyond even words—is also thwarted, unfulfilled; men instead live at odds with their brothers—"the Lord confused the language of all the earth. . ." (Gen. 11:9).

That's the great danger, when the things of this world, loved and reverenced in their own right, are not taken up and offered in the hands of love. And it's a constant threat to our current art, our current science, our current technology, that it will become for us an idolatry and end in the ruin of itself and in the shattering of human community.

So much depends on who handles, who offers the things of this world, and in what spirit he offers them. I commend to you, in your materialism, the example of the love found at the wedding in Cana—love materialized, love incarnate, himself loving the things he handles, himself taking them up and offering them in the concern of love. Perhaps for you that example is the ultimate argument, the ultimate explanation of every gift, every action: I do it because love tells me to, because Jesus the Lord tell me to. . . .

Now this is third: the materialism that I commend to you offers its gifts for the sake of the beloved. The gift, the action, the word, these are offered to the brother for his sake, according to his need.

So, for instance, at the wedding party the wine fails, the guests will be disappointed, the party will be a flop, and for the sake of these others—his mother, his disciples, the wedding host, the wedding guests—for the sake of these Jesus offers his gift. At first there is some reluctance: "What have you to do with me? My hour has not yet come. . ." And then, changing his mind, as it were, there is the spirit of good times, the spirit of rejoicing with those who rejoice. Well, why not? "Having gifts that differ according to the grace given to us, let us use them . . ." (Romans 12:6). I suggest to you that this materialism uses its gifts in the service of the beloved, to fill his needs, his wants.

And I know from the start the dangers in this approach. This attitude could degenerate into a supercilious patronizing. It could become very self-righteous. These are the dangers, and in the past century we've seen the results of that kind of patronizing self-righteousness in the church's overseas mission fields. You know, the white-man's-burden kind of attitude that says, quite literally, "I'm going to give you this for your own good, by God." And you read the sorry record of Christian missionaries who dress the south seas natives in muumuus, and teach them to eat their cocoanut with knife and fork and spoon. I don't mean that kind of thing. What I do mean is this: a kind of simple, elemental humanism, if you want to use the term; the kind of humanism displayed when one starving beggar tells a second starving beggar where to find food.

And I stress the personal, humanistic focus of this materialism—that it gives its gifts solely for the sake of the one who's loved—simply by way of contrast with the other option. The fact is, the non-materialist is apt to put his focus elsewhere, not in human need but in, say, spiritual values, or because it's a matter of principle, or because of some ethical system, or because of some theological or doctrinal position, or because of some moral code. Now I have great respect for principles, and spiritual values, and theology, and doctrine, and moral codes, and all the rest. As a Lutheran I'd rather cut my throat than give up a favorite doctrinal position (and frequently have!). But as a Christian materialist I have to be ready to sacrifice all these, if necessary, for the sake of human need.

As I say, for me personally, that's not an easy thing to do. But the New Testament teaches me that love sometimes makes that demand. And love can make that demand only within the context of a community of faith, only within that relationship to my Father and to my brothers which is based on the confidence of forgiveness. The Christian materialist gives his gifts not because of principles of a higher good, not because of an ethical system or a theological position, but simply because his neighbor needs them. And that giving is liable not to be cheap, not to be easy. It is liable to cost him something.

While my wife was in the hospital last week, I read J. D. Salinger's *Franny and Zooey*[2]. I'm serving notice that you will probably get sick of hearing me talk about this book, but I think it is rather special. The book is about a screwball family in New York City named Glass, where, rarely enough in modern fiction, the members really love each other. Franny, the daughter in the family, has come home from college in a kind of nervous breakdown, full of religious mysticism and emotional tension, and simply remains lying on the living room sofa, refusing to eat or drink, refusing any comfort or conversation. Her mother, Bessie, exhibits the kind of human focus I'm talking about when she brings her daughter a bowl of chicken soup. Every ten minutes she brings it, and it's driving her daughter nuts, but it's in a concern of love and Franny knows it. Here her daughter hasn't eaten in twenty-four hours. What does Franny need? thinks Bessie. She needs a nice hot cup of chicken soup, that's what she needs. And Bessie gives it even though she won't accept it. And even though she won't admit it, Franny gets the message.

Well, this is last, in defense of materialism: After all this, the mystery takes place. First the gift, loved and reverenced in its own right, taken up and offered in the hands of love, offered to the beloved for his sake, for his service; then the mystery, and the material becomes more than material, the earthly becomes more than earthly, more than

[2] J. D. Salinger, *Franny and Zooey* (Boston: Little, Brown and Co., 1961).

of this world. It becomes sacramental, truly holy, with all the powers of heaven contained within.

This is the pattern of incarnation, the pattern of sacrament, where the things of this world, the common, humble, "secular", physical things of this world are now suddenly vehicles for a heavenly invasion, with power to bind up and forgive and accept and make new, power to mediate between God and man, between man and his brother, power to give everlasting life. And what was once tasteless water now still remains water, yet also has become the wine of life.

Something like this ought to happen to you in the giving of your gifts at the altar, at the Offertory, where in our worship we have the chance to respond in gratitude to all that our Lord has done for us. Your tainted money, your limited gifts, your meager talents, your insufficient time, all that makes up *you*, when offered in this spirit becomes sacramental, truly rich, truly holy. Something like this ought to happen to you every time you handle the things of this world.

There's a notable passage in Salinger's book. Franny is still pining away on the sofa in her combined emotional collapse and religious mysticism, but she listens to the counsel of her older brother Zooey as he bawls her out, tells her her religion is all wet. He says, "You're missing out on every single religious action that's going on around this house. You don't even have sense enough to drink when someone brings you a cup of consecrated chicken soup—which is the only kind of chicken soup Bessie ever brings to anybody around this madhouse. . ."[3]

I like that image: consecrated chicken soup, chicken soup

[3] *Ibid.*, p. 194.

now made holy, chicken soup participating in the nature of sacrament. Part of my job among you is to witness to the fact that I have seen this happen; I have seen this happen.

I have tasted consecrated chicken soup. I daresay when you were a child and skinned your knee, you felt the comfort of a consecrated band-aid. Perhaps now that you have lived awhile on campus you have smoked a consecrated cigarette, seen a consecrated smile or wink, felt a consecrated handshake. My infant daughter, Anna Ruth, has already known the change of a consecrated diaper.

Now that may be materialism but it is also sacramental. And it traces the pattern of incarnation, when God who is love became man for the sake of men, became physical man for the sake of physical men. And the pattern of this event changes and consecrates everything you touch, every atom, every gift, every word, every action.

NINE

Communion and Emotion

GILBERT E. DOAN, JR.

IT'S JUST ABOUT IMPOSSIBLE
to come thoughtfully to a Service of Holy Communion
and not be plagued by a host of unanswered—and perhaps
unanswerable—questions:

What effect should this have on me?

How much depends on my attitude?

In what sense is God really present here, especially "in"
the elements?

What connection does this little ceremony have with
that historical "last" supper, there in the upper room?

Did Jesus, at that point, really command all this
repetition?

Why should the Holy Communion, of all things, stand
as a barrier between denominations—or between Lutherans, for that matter?

What connection is there between this eating and drinking and that uneasy moment yesterday when I snubbed a
good friend because I was trying to impress someone else?

These are all vital questions, of course. But there's another one that keeps raising its head. It's an especially
troublesome question. Perhaps you've asked it yourself.
It's not the kind of question that used to enrage the ama-

teur atheists (you know: *"How* can bread and wine be *changed* into body and blood?") It's of the duller, nagging sort that bothers Christians—so badly, sometimes, that they can't quite admit it, even to themselves. It goes something like this: "When I was confirmed, and time came for the first Communion, I was so keyed up, I was sure everybody could see my knees knocking. I was afraid I'd faint on the spot! It was a real emotional trauma. But somehow it's not the same any more. I don't seem to be emotionally affected at all these days. As if my heart weren't in it. It doesn't seem to mean what it used to. I wonder whether I really ought to go at all if I can't take it seriously."

Now, of course, this is in the mood of the day: a mood of self-analysis, a determination not to have anything to do with phony emotions, and a kind of wistful desperation because authentic, compelling emotions are not, apparently, to be had in quantity. Contemporary literature is governed to a large degree by this mood, from *The Stranger* of Camus, whose chief character, having murdered a man, is judged guilty not because he took another's life, but because he did not show the proper emotional strain at his mother's funeral—from this familiar stranger to Holden Caulfield, the schoolboy of Salinger's *Catcher in the Rye,* whose life is one long response of perpetual nausea to the phoniness he sees in his parents, his teachers, his classmates. This is the figure of the man of today, his face sophisticated, serene, skilled in the suppression of any deep emotion—to say nothing of the phony—while if you look at his feet you find them shuffling painfully, wistfully, groping secretly and clumsily, feeling for the bedrock of life.

That's a picture of us in our time, and it's small wonder that at the Lord's table we're asking ourselves, "It's not really the same any more; should I really be here at all?"

This is only a part of the story of our concern for the relationship between the Communion and our emotional response. It is the part that we share with all the men and women of our day. But we are also the people of the church. Are there perhaps also *religious* roots beneath this anxious, often wordless concern? I think there are, and digging into a bit of history may help us to expose them.

For one, our church has always laid heavy stress on "worthy" reception, remembering the words of St. Paul, "He that eateth and drinketh unworthily eateth and drinketh damnation unto himself" (I Cor. 11:27, AV)—which is true, of course, of the Communion, just as it is of any other of the myriad ways in which God chooses to confront us. Even so, Paul's warning is frightening, and it's not surprising that we feel we should take Communion seriously.

Now, there are two ways, at least, of encouraging people to take something like this seriously. One is to help people to learn how to receive, and to provide plenty of opportunities for the exercise of right receiving, so that they may approach this gift with something like faith and confidence. The other is to provide so few such occasions that men and women are scared into seriousness. Luther pretty generally recommended the first way. Our churches in this country, however, have unfortunately chosen, by and large, the second. The logic is pretty wobbly, but it gets results: people have indeed been worked up into a sort of fearful, traumatic respect for the sacrament of the altar. Obviously, however, this sort of emotion wears thin after a time, and it should then come as no shock to us that even the respect is not the same.

There is another strand in the history of the church that helps us to understand this problem of Communion and emotion. It is a truism that every revolution has a reaction, and that revolution called the "Reformation" was no exception. The reaction to the Reformation was what is now called the "orthodoxism" of 17th century Lutheran theology. Many theologians were then reverting to the cold, rationalistic doctrinal perfectionism which had characterized the pre-Reformation church. Some of our concern for doctrinally "worthy" reception has its source in this era.

Then there was a reaction against orthodoxism. It was called "pietism," and the gist of it was that it didn't really matter too much exactly what you believed, as long as the warm glow of piety was to be seen. Some of our concern today is a hangover from this period, too. If a Christian can be identified by his fervor, then, it would seem we ought to go to and whomp up the fervor.

The trouble is that the only really convincing state of mind we can work ourselves into is that of remorse. And that's one reason the Communion has for so many people become a gloomy, somber, morose affair, rather than the joyous eucharist, or thanksgiving, the life-giving encounter with God that it was meant to be. This kind of remorsefulness is what Kierkegaard describes as ". . . selfish, a matter of the senses, sensually powerful for the moment, excited in expression . . . —and, just on this account, is not real repentance. [It] would drink down all the bitterness of sorow in a single draught and then hurry on. It wants to get away from guilt . . .—and then . . . hurry on.[1]

[1] Soren Kierkegaard, *Purity of Heart*, translated by Douglas V. Steere. (New York: Harper, 1948.) p. 44.

This kind of remorseful mood we can work ourselves in-to, but I doubt it is pleasing to God. I doubt that our Lord is much flattered by our attempts to simulate the proper emotions. Do you remember the woman who got herself all carried away and cried out, "Blessed is the womb that bore thee and the paps which thou hast sucked"? (Which, being interpreted, is, "how lucky your mother is to have such a fine boy!) And you remember his reply, "Yea, rather blessed are they that hear the word of God and keep it" (Luke 11:27-28, AV).

If now you weave together these two strands of history (each of them important and each in a sense altogether right), this concern for worthy reception from the ortho-doxists and the pietists' preoccupation with *visible* emo-tional and spiritual warmth, you come out with an equation of sorts:

> If you receive worthily . . .
> . . . you will have the right emotions.

Which is all true, in a special sense. But somehow we have gotten the reaction reversed and inverted, and it now reads differently. (It comes out in a form, incidentally, which you might just have to stretch a bit to conform with "justi-fication by grace alone. . .") Now it seems to read:

> If you don't come away with (what you think are)
>   the right emotions . . .
> Then you are not worthy to receive.

—as though any man or woman were! As though this sac-rament were not intended precisely for the special comfort and strengthening of sinful and unworthy people!

For if Luther said one thing, if the New Testament says one thing, if that distilled essence of the New Testament, the Creed, says one thing about God, it is this: that he acted, and acts to save us, to make us his own, all by himself, and that no pious work that we do, and no pious emotion that we can dutifully wring from our reluctant, narrow, sluggish hearts can make us one gram more worthy of his love and his concern for us.

And when a man first *learns* this, to be sure, his step is lighter, his eye brighter—just as in the early stages of a courtship merely to be in the presence of the other is to be consumed as with sweet fire. But are those newlyweds not bound for trouble unless they are prepared to come down after the wedding trip from the mount of romantic transfiguration? Come down they inevitably must; and if they are not prepared to give up the honeymoon glow, they are going to feel frustrated, cheated, bilked. Happy that man and woman who are prepared to stop looking for the consuming thrill of romance, who are prepared instead to be not consumed, but nourished and strengthened by the deep, quiet love and devotion that come only with the months and the years. So with Christmas. First the Santa Claus stage, then the trains and dolls stage, then the Yuletide party stage. And then . . . what happens? You hear this: "I just don't seem to have the old Christmas spirit any more." It doesn't mean you're getting senile just because your rompers and your playsuit don't fit you any more. It only means you're ready for something bigger, more mature. So with the Holy Communion. As you come to the table, think on these things.

Again, someone has said that there is insincerity in every attempt to be sincere. To us who have just confessed to sinfulness in thought, word, and deed, this observation should come as no great shock. Was that confession one hundred percent sincere? I submit that you and I confessed because, among other things, we are rarely, if ever, one hundred percent sincere. Indeed, that's one reason *why* we make a confession. It surely would do us doubtful good to try, by confessing, to prove to God (of all people) that we were sincere; even less to strain toward being sincere. If there were any future in that, making a confession would be wasting valuable time. But the point is that we *can't* do anything about it. We *are* that way. That's why we make confession—and ask *God* to do something about it. (And of course the dangerous part of it is that he just might do that. . .) I submit that it's a good thing God doesn't measure out his grace according to the measure of the sincerity you and I have been able to muster up in confession. Fortunately he knows our insincerity a good deal better than we do. You and I confess only to avoid the other alternative—the one Adam chose, there in Eden; the Lord God asked him simple, pointed questions—actually the Lord God was just pleading with him to confess— and Adam responded by passing the buck. We confess, then, because we would like to avoid at least that.

God comes to us, then, not because we make such sincere confession, but just because we are insincere, and know it, and want to be otherwise. So we make the best and most honest confession we can, and we leave the rest —including the emotions—in his hands. When you come to the table, think on these things.

Yet not on these alone, for these are still about ourselves, our factual insincerity and our growing maturity that does not go on expecting the same kinds of emotions as we remember from confirmation.

But think, too, on other things. Think of the millions,

across the mountains and the seas, who today will share with you this gift of God. Think especially of those who, because of tribulation in their lands, come to the altar as to life itself, when all the rest of what used to be called their life has lost its meaning. Think of those to whom simply to be found at the altar of God may mean death. Pray for them, and ask God to give them, indeed, that special comfort and strengthening.

And think of this God who filled the primordial silence with voices and with music, who rolled back the curtains of the darkness and flung out a fistful of stars for beauty and for a witness.

Think of the holy one of Israel whose train filled the temple, before whose presence the angels veil their faces, whose name brings men to their knees in wonder and in awe.

Finally think of this God coming among us as a man, born human so that we could know him and have a way to understand his will and his love for us. A man, as common-ordinary as bread, who knew our suffering and for us spilled his own blood like wine, who gave himself to us on a common cross and now gives himself to us in common bread and wine to tell us he wants us even on our common days and in our unexalted, painful moods.

Think on these things. Think about him. And lift up your hearts!

TEN

When You Are Young
You See Things Separately

RICHARD QUENTIN ELVEE

When you are young you see things separately.
Yesterday in the Science Hall
I saw a butterfly
transfixed on a pin.
And I thought of all the butterflies
in the dusty halls of colleges,
sitting erect in their cabinets of glass;
spoils of the scientist
who netted their brief flight,
pinned their thin thread breath on wood
and stamped them with his words,
nymphalidae, hesperidae, metazoa, insecta,
caught and classified,
and stored away in a little corner of his experience.
When you are young you see things separately.
Nature stands alone.
But after a while, you will understand that things join
    together;
that man falls into nature, and nature into man.
This is the secret of the butterfly—it holds a part of man,

and man contains the butterfly. This is the mystery of the
 butterfly
and the man. They come from a single hand. They share
 a world.

They share a world—a September afternoon of another
 year, when the
butterfly yellow with autumn danced along the sweet
 smelling bushes
behind Old Main, and the boy chased the thing, all wing
 and dance and color.

They share a world—the sadness in things—mortality.
 Men, like butterflies
caught on autumn afternoons by death, before nightful
 replaced by
myriad others, who crawl from life's womb to stand in the
 long rays
of the sun.

They share a world—its loneliness and longing.
"Before the door, where you went away,
each footprint is overgrown with green moss
So deep it is none can sweep it away,
the first autumn wind added the falling leaves.
And now in September, yellowing butterflies
hover two by two in our west garden grasses.
And because of all this, my heart is breaking,
and I fear for my bright cheeks lest they fade." [1]

[1] Li Po, tr. by Witter Bynner from the texts of Kiang Kang-hu. *The
Wisdom of China and India*, Lin Yutang, ed. (New York: Modern
Library, 1955). p. 903.

Ah when you are young you see things separately. After a
　while
they join together, nature and man, and . . . God.

On mornings like this in late summer, when I sit in the
　chapel, waiting
for the service to begin. Sometimes a butterfly will flutter
　along
outside the glass, like a piece of yellow paper in the wind.
　And I wonder
to myself, how it is that such little things in this world
　should move
beside the big, a tiny insect beside temples and organs and
　all of the
large, large words we use here—God, Death and
　Immortality.

Perhaps—they belong together.

O it may be they have brought to men the colors of
　paradise, wings
that bear the tulip's fire, the sheen of cherry blossoms, the
　delicate
canvasses of yellow suns which set in a world he lost as
　the gates fell
which shut him out forever. It may be that as he took the
　difficult road,
an angel pitied him and sent a host of butterflies to follow
　him into
exile. They came about him out of the hedges of the
　garden, and he knew
them by the magic of their hues.

So man tilled the earth, and the butterflies multiplied over
the plains.
Sometimes one of them would brush past a stooping toiler,
and lure him
to follow where it led. And he would straighten his back,
gaze after
the bright beckoner and see again the gold hedge of
paradise.

And the butterflies spread and spread over the earth.
The night the ovens were lit at Auschwitz,
they moaned in the tall autumn grasses,
and all of the long summer after Jesus died,
struggled and struggled out of cocoons,
in the soft morning light
When you are young you see things separately. After a
while,
they join together, and roll in a great procession about the
Central Light.

93

ELEVEN

A Time of Silence
in Your Soul

PAUL J. HOH

ASH WEDNESDAY

ASH. ASHES AND DESTRUCTION and the great gray silence of death. Sackcloth and ashes, the rending of clothes, a time of mourning, a time of repentence, the great gray silence of the soul.

This is a time to be silent, to fall prostrate at the foot of the altar and hear with trembling heart the voice: "Be still and know that I am God," (Psalms 46:10).

If we would know the meaning of repentance, we must be willing to be alone. To be sure, there is a time and a place for public confession. There is a grace given in the baring of one's soul before a brother in Christ. There is a corporate character to the guilt which we bear as a people, as a nation, as a race—as humanity itself. But to plumb the depths of our own sin and guilt means to turn our eyes rigorously upon ourselves, our motives, our uncontrolled emotions, our own complacency, our own stopped-up ears, shut eyes, tight-fisted hands, the hardness of our hearts and

the softness of our thinking. . . The dark road of repentance we must walk alone. There is a solitary night of the
soul that must precede the dawn and there we can find
ourselves, see ourselves, take stock of ourselves—in solitude and silence.

Our scientists construct rooms in which it is possible to
attain almost absolute silence. They say it is an unearthly
feeling to sit in such a room. The places you and I call
quiet rage with sound compared to these perfectly insulated
rooms. There is an initial reaction akin to terror when *all*
sound ceases, and then, when the person has adjusted to
this strange new environment, a new sound is heard. It is
the flow of blood through the blood vessels in the ear. You
can't hear that now—though the sound is there. But if all
the other distracting noises of this place were stilled completely, you could learn to hear your own blood coursing
through your ears.

Does God speak louder than that tiny sound—not to the
inner ear, of course, but to the inner man? Is his whisper
audible over the distracting sounds of turmoil in our minds
and hearts? Or must we learn to listen with just such con-
centration, such determined exclusion of the competing
voices of this life? To listen in what may be for us a new
environment, an absolute silence of the spirit? It may even
take time to adjust to the terror of such stillness within.

But should this surprise us? Why should we expect that
the presence of the holy God is going to be as obvious to
our eyes as the physical structures with which man crowds
the landscape. As overpowering to our ears as the strident
advertising which fills our airwaves, invades our homes,
adds to the din of supermarkets, captures the car radio and
swells the roar of traffic? Is God going to wage a saturation

campaign of 30-second spot advertisements on TV and radio?

It was not the earthquake, not the rushing wind, not the roar of fire which bore the voice of God—it was the still, the small voice of calm.

Brother Lawrence spoke of the "practice of the presence of God"—and we're insulted that God would expect us to practice, to work at . . . listening. We seem to be convinced, though we'd deny the words, that we're doing God a favor by believing in him, so we regard it as the supreme affront that this one whom we are so good-naturedly willing to serve should turn around and ask more of us. But the gifts he would give us come only through open doors—he asks only that we be willing to let the doors be opened.

We come to commune with God, to have communication with him—not just this night, but in all the days and weeks before us. How easily we can assume that communication demands sound instead of silence; words instead of the word.

Even in our relationships with other people we know how often the words we say are simply a cloak in which to hide ourselves from each other. Our music, especially today, instead of being a "universal language," may simply provide a protective covering for impersonal relationships. We sit in the same rooms, sometimes live in the same families, as strangers. We may say that the fault is that we don't talk to each other, but really the problem is that we don't listen to each other, not to the person behind the words, not to the lonely silence behind the face.

So even with each other we need at times the ministry of silence, certainly a willingness of at least one to be silent, to still his own thoughts long enough to hear, really to hear, the person who sits there so unknown.

If this is true with people with flesh and blood like ours, with others who share the life of this world in which we, too, are set, whom we should understand just from knowing ourselves, whose language should communicate because it is also our language, whose fears and hopes and dreams and despair are all the accents of our own past and present and future . . . then how much more listening is needed to hear God's word to us.

Lay aside, then, in this silence before God, all other things. Let neither desire or despair, earthly fortune or earthly care, intrude upon the solitude of your repentance. Hear as if for the first time the impossible yet utterly true message of his love and salvation which he is speaking to you in the liturgy of the Communion. Come to his table with a heart tuned only to his voice. And let this be the beginning of a time of silence in your soul, the practice of his presence through the long way we travel here in Lent.

TWELVE

Self-Control

ROBERT W. JENSON

NOTE: This sermon is from a series on "The Fruits of the Spirit."

But the fruit of the Spirit is . . . self-control. . .
—*Galatians 5:22-23*

PAUL'S LIST IS ANTICLIMACTIC
—after such glorious, bubbling
gifts as joy, faithfulness, love, he finishes with a dull,
bourgeois, spiritless virtue like "self-control." Indeed, it
appears that he has lifted this virtue from similar lists
    made
by the Stoics, those grimmest and most romantic of
    killjoys.
"Self-control" means nothing-too-much; it is the absence of
ectstasy.
Why?
With this gift God recognizes that our life much of the
    time *is*
dull, bourgeois and unromantic—and stoops to bless this
    also.

98

Springs of joy, moments of peace, acts of kindness—these
are
relatively rare in our lives. Most of life is getting up and
reading what we'd rather not and eating what's put there
and
seeing the same people as yesterday.

We may ourselves have made life so, but that does not
change it.

And in these long stretches of nothing-much-in-particular,
the
gift needed is just this nothing-much-in-particular virtue—
Knowing how to stop eating when you've had enough.
Knowing when and how to put the brakes on the regular
Saturday date.
Making yourself study instead of joining the bull-session,
if that's
what's called for.

This is the gift needed,
If life is not to explode, not with joy but with hell.

God gives us this gift.

He is not interested in our great moments only,
In our black sins and glorious joys.
He has made himself the sharer of *all* our life, including
our everyday.
He has eaten restaurant food and talked day after day to
the same
people and stopped for traffic signs—

And in all this humdrum he has exercised self-control.

In all the things of our life he took what was available,
And enjoyed it,
And went on—
In order that nothing should distract him from loving us.
When we gave him no bed, he didn't complain.
When we crucified him, he forgave us.
When we ignore his love, he keeps right on.
When we do not listen to his word, he repeats it.

Therefore we can do the same.
In all the long stretches of eating and sleeping and
    nothing-much-
in-particular we are sharing *Jesus'* life and moving toward
    reunion
with him.

And so there is no need to eat too much or love too soon or
    day-dream
too long.
There is no need to burst out in order to put a little
    excitement
into life.
Life has, *just as* the humdrum it is, all the excitement of
    God.

THIRTEEN

There's Glory for You

RICHARD LUECKE

On the third day there was a marriage at Cana in Galilee, and the mother of Jesus was there; Jesus also was invited to the marriage, with his disciples. When the wine failed, the mother of Jesus said to him, "They have no wine." And Jesus said to her, "O woman, what have you to do with me? My hour has not yet come." His mother said to the servants, "Do whatever he tells you." Now six stone jars were standing there, for the Jewish rites of purification, each holding twenty or thirty gallons. Jesus said to them, "Fill the jars with water." And they filled them up to the brim. He said to them, "Now draw some out, and take it to the steward of the feast." So they took it. When the steward of the feast tasted the water now become wine, and did not know where it came from (though the servants who had drawn the water knew), the steward of the feast called the bridegroom and said to him, "Every man serves the good wine first; and when men have drunk freely, then the poor wine; but you have kept the good wine until now." This, the first of his signs, Jesus did at Cana in Galilee, and manifested his glory; and his disciples believed in him.

—John 2:1-11

101

". . . There's glory for you!"

"I don't know what you mean by 'glory,' " Alice said.

Humpty Dumpty smiled contemptuously. "Of course you don't—till I tell you. I meant 'there's a nice knock-down argument for you!' "

"But 'glory' doesn't mean 'a nice knockdown argument,' " Alice objected.

"When I use a word," Humpty Dumpty said, in rather *a scornful tone, "it means just what I choose it to mean—neither more nor less."*

"The question is," said Alice, *"whether you* can *make words mean so many different things."*

"The question is," said Humpty Dumpty, *"which is to be master—that's all."*

Through the Looking Glass, *Chapter VI*

THE WORD FOR THESE EPIPHANY days is "glory." The question before us is whether we are people who have any use for this word (or any glory in our lives) and, if so, what it is that we mean by it. We might, if we wished, spend our time finding traces of this word in our ordinary speech: in our talk about a glorious sunset, or the glories of the nation ("Old Glory"), or opera, or basketball, or even find echoes in trade names like Halo Shampoo. But let's go at once to the Gospel of John and find the meaning of glory there. The question is, "Who is to be the master?"—that's all.

The master here is Jesus of Nazareth, and the story is the wedding at Cana. It is important that this "first of his signs" should have been given at a wedding, and an un-expectedly gay one at that. The wine has run out. Now this is hardly what we sober spirits would call a crisis—at least not the kind of crisis we customarily refer to Christ. I once heard an older clergyman say on college career day that the function of the church is to "preside over the crises of life." By "crises" he meant mostly failures and misfortunes like delinquency, divorce, sickness, and death. If we had believed him, then we who felt far removed from such problems might have filed the church, and perhaps even Christ, away for future reference. At least in practice, many appear to agree that religion is for a time of trouble, rather than for a time of joy. Christ is invited to sickbeds and funerals, rather than to parties or celebrations. Yet, today we find him not at the bed of Simon's mother, nor at the tomb of Lazarus, but at the wedding of Cana. The question arises for all of us: does Christ stand only at life's extremities? Does he go only to men who are sick or old or at the end of their tether? No, says this Gospel, Christ also stands in the center of life with the competent, the young, the movers of society, where the blood is running and the sap is rising. There is a kind of "crisis" in the strengths and joys of life where Christ may manifest his glory.

What Jesus does here is called a "sign." A sign is something right in front of our eyes which points to something which is not simply a matter of physical sight. The people in the Gospels were always asking Jesus for a sign—a "sign from heaven" to show that he really was, as they said, "from God." A "sign" would do this in two ways: by calling attention to the *one* who performed it, and by calling attention to *what* he was doing, to something of which the action itself was a striking and memorable instance though that something would have to be clarified by speech. This is clear from the whole structure of the Gospel of John which proceeds as a kind of "book of signs:" a series of significant actions, each followed by a discourse or a discussion or a controversy over something which did not simply meet the eye but which was really at issue in those actions. The discourse which follows this sign is the memorable one with Nicodemus. In that conversation we find words which unfold what is signified by this action—which try to say what it means for all other circumstances that water set apart in the six stone jars for rites of purification, is turned by Christ into the best wine of Cana.

Let's stay with this picture of the celebration of a marriage. We still seek to preserve marriage, and even to govern romance, through certain "rites of purification"—that is, by laws and morals and customs and by self-discipline and self-control. We deceive ourselves if we imagine we can do without such controls. Least of all, perhaps, in the matter of physical love which is unusually able to distract us from work or study or other valuable forms of community and enjoyment. This desire is more distracting or monopolizing, for example, than the desire for food. (Someone has observed that not even the most passionate gourmet would buy a ticket to watch a lid get removed by stages from a beef steak and, while saxophones blare, shout "take it off.")

And yet rules and disciplines place a heavy and seemingly contradictory burden on desire and love which, in themselves, do not wish to be caged. Love cannot be confined to a pattern. The waywardness of love is part of its very nature. If it did not seek to leap every barrier, if it could be tamed, love would not be the creative force we know it to be and want it to be. *The Scarlet Letter* depicts both this essential freedom and necessary discipline in

Hester Prynne, the wearer of the scarlet letter. There she lives, and has to live, in that cabin at the edge of town, behind which stretches the virgin wilderness (where on one springtime occasion the story began), and in front of which lies the Puritan village with the laws and morals and customs within which she needs to move. Love and desire pushing from behind and controls standing arms akimbo in front. Nathaniel Hawthorne very wisely leaves this problem unsolved, for it cannot be solved by a simple choice between the two. All we get is the grace and hope imparted by Hester Prynne herself to those who come to her for counsel because they have had too much romance or too little love or (as is often the case) both.

Other stories unfold the problem by showing us someone who makes a choice. Amy in *Summer and Smoke* obeys all the rules or puts out only a toe to passion—but in the end she knows she has denied something of life. Don Giovanni breaks the rules and follows his passions, but this, too, proves self-defeating. The trouble is not merely that his behavior is unacceptable to others who, therefore, seek to punish or destroy him; most of those in the story who take exception to his freely esthetic behavior are less acceptable to the viewer than he is and they fail much less heroically. The trouble, finally, is that Giovanni's behavior makes impossible the very relationship he seeks. Seduction plays at love but denies personality—which love implies. Girls are people too.

There are magazines which pretend this is not so complicated as it is. One of them proposes a "playmate of the month" which can be folded out and then folded back in again. The idea is appealing, especially to beginners in such relationships, because it *is* very difficult to conjoin passion and person. Denis de Rougemont, a learned French commentator, describes most sharply a familiar incompatability between "romance" and "marriage": one requires the repeated absence, the other requires the perpetual presence of the one loved.

> By its very nature, romance is incompatible with marriage (even if it provokes it), for it is essentially nourished by obstacles, delays, separation, and dreams, while marriage essentially must reduce or suppress these obstacles every day, must be realized in the immediate and in constant physical closeness. . . Marriage kills romance, and if romance is reborn it will kill marriage for the same reasons for which the marriage took place.[1]

That is how we find ourselves when Christ breaks in upon the scene—when the story of Cana comes to us as a sign of his redeeming work and its proper effect. The "glory" which this gospel announced at its very outset was that of one who was "full of grace and truth." Christ not only revealed the truth about life—what life ought to be like, but is not. He also revealed that truth in a way which beckoned, which related men to that truth in spite of their failure. He brought the "forgiveness of sins." This forgiveness is more than principle or premise; it is an action. It frees us from something, for something. In terms of our present topic, it frees us from seeking and serving ourselves in romance and marriage. We are always in danger of seeking to "save ourselves" in this way. The coed laments, "I came to be went with but I haven't gone yet." Full grown adults look to marriage to solve their problems— but learn soon enough that marriage creates as many prob-

[1] Denis de Rougemont, *The Christian Opportunity* (New York: Holt, Rinehart and Winston, 1961), p. 95.

lems as it solves. The first meaning of this "sign" is that we are not saved *by* romance or *by* marriage—but that we may be saved *for* it.

We are saved to be *for* one another. In the warmth of romance, to be sure, we always imagine we are, naturally and emotionally, for the other. But such feelings are very undependable, as may be learned each time those feelings diminish or turn to hatred when we feel ourselves deprived by the other. The point of the gospel is that we are saved to be for the other as he is in Christ, as having a freedom and a future of his own. We are saved for a marriage which has its own proper purpose in the world.

That is why we accept institutions and laws, morals and customs. How else can we be sure that the proper being of the partner is safeguarded, seeing we ourselves are so undependable? And that the purpose of marriage is safeguarded, though that purpose is threatened by petulant romance? But now rules and restraints are no longer a burden. They are *instruments*. Christ always waits to turn the water of social-control and self-discipline into the wine of gladness. At the close of his *Christmas Oratorio*, W. H. Auden speaks of how we return from the celebration of Christ's birth to the routines of life. But there is a difference, if we look beyond them to him.

He is the Life.

Love Him in the World of the Flesh,

And at your marriage all its occasions shall dance
for joy.[2]

Something similar could be said about our use of wine.

[2] From "For the Time Being," copyright 1944 by W. H. Auden. Reprinted from *The Collected Poetry of W. H. Auden*, by permission of Random House, Inc.

We are all familiar with the "rite of purification" in this matter. One generation tries prohibition, a legal solution to this problem. The next generation decides to refer this problem to self-discipline or self-control. Both solutions often fail, and this is a matter of profound regret to anyone who has seen careers, marriages, homes, bodies, minds, broken in this way. But something more needs to be said than simply to compare the alternatives of legal prohibition and self-control. Neither really touches the heart of the matter. On the one hand, a man craves to feel grand because in one sense he is grand. He was brought forth, says James, to be "a kind of first fruits of his creatures" (1:18). On the other hand, he needs to numb the senses which tell him he is not so simply grand at all—in order to defy or forget the walls of guilt and death which press in on every side. Laws and disciplines are only reminders of those walls unless we are pointed to something more than legal and more than moral. Unless the waters of life can be turned into something stronger and deeper. . .

Christ did not come merely to solve our ethical or social problems. He came "that they may have life, and have it abundantly" (John 10:11). The New Testament does not merely lay down a law, it offers a gift: "Do not get drunk with wine . . . but be filled with the Spirit" (Eph. 5:18). Both of these things are included in the picture of the best wine of Cana: freedom *from* seeking to save ourselves with wine, freedom *for* a thankful and joyful use of wine. "Whether you eat or drink, or whatever you do, do all to the glory of God" (I Cor. 10:31).

There is a "crisis of abundance," as we all know, in our society at this time. Technological advance not only promises an end of grinding labor and basic goods for all, it is also producing "technological unemployment" and a new dependency in the poor. Large scale corporate activity not only brings efficiency to certain major projects, it also removes from most people any share in the decisions which affect their lives—from baseball to warfare, concerning the products they use or the services they get or the entertainment they enjoy. This means, once again, the need for regulatory agencies or controls. It imposes on everyone a new demand for political participation by which men order and control the technical and social forces which control their lives.

Sometimes it's said that there's a crisis of faith in the new abundance. When all are fed and housed and clothed, where will be the need for faith? If we remember the wedding at Cana, however, we might see such a state of affairs as the very occasion of a new birth of faith. When men no longer die of hunger or thirst, or exposure or disease, and the only thing men die of is death itself, they may confront more clearly the issue of faith itself. There will, moreover, be the need for the most basic act of faith of all: the act of thanksgiving, the sacrifice of praise. The kingdom of heaven is described as filled with praise. He manifests his glory when the vessels overflow.

Desire and control, which once seemed the sum of life and the struggle of life, are now seen to point beyond themselves to something that is more than either and more than both—to something in which desire and control are united and where "glory" is to be found. To understand this fully we would need to follow the career of this word "glory" through the Gospel of John. Remember Jesus' words to his mother in this story: "My hour has not yet come." We encounter these words again and again in the course of this Gospel. Sometimes when his enemies were enraged and took up stones or sought to push him over a cliff, he left the scene unharmed because "his hour had not yet come" (7:20; 8:31-39). What was that great hour to which it all pointed, which would most fully manifest his glory? When at last that hour comes, it is a strange one indeed: it is the "hour" of his passion and death. "What shall I say, 'Father, save me from this hour'? No, for this purpose I have come to this hour. Father, glorify thy name" (12:27). "Father, the hour has come . . . glorify thy Son that the Son may glorify thee" (17:1). Lest we imagine that this "glory" refers only to the suffering and death of Christ himself, Jesus says that the glory which had been given him he has given to the disciples (17:22). Lest we imagine this imparted glory refers to behavior which is very different, or only to a world which is still to come, Jesus tells Peter "by what death *he* was to glorify God" (21:18-19).

Beyond desire is passion. Beyond discipline is discipleship. There is a glory to be found in all of life: at a wedding or in a cross. It is the point of the Gospel that if glory was present in a cross then it can be present in a wedding. It is the point of this lesson that unless we find glory in a wedding, we may never find it in a cross. Grace frees us to enter into both, each in its own time. The book of Ecclesiastes speaks of "a time for every matter under heaven: a time to be born and a time to die . . . a time to mourn, and a time to dance . . . a time to embrace, and a time to refrain from embracing" (3:1-8). The trouble with most of us is that we mourn when we should dance and dance when we should mourn; we don't know when to embrace or when to refrain from embracing, and know neither how to live nor how to die. We try to have everything at once, as Bonhoeffer said: "Matrimonial bliss and the cross and the heavenly Jerusalem—where there is neither marriage nor giving in marriage."

We have before us today a sign very like the one in our lesson. The elements are bread and wine: bread which betokens and accompanies life's most basic toils; wine which betokens and often accompanies life's highest joys. Christ waits to enter both. This bread and this wine will be used to show forth Christ's death. But we will do a surprising thing. We will suround that sign of his death with words of thanksgiving and songs of glory. "It is truly meet, right, and salutary that we should at all times and in all places give thanks. . !" "Heaven and earth are full of thy glory!" At a time when men are sick or disturbed because of conflicts between desire and control, someone had better remember to give thanks. At a time when the best efforts of society go into seeking prosperity and keeping order, someone had better remember to sing of glory.

There is glory for you, though this is a surprising new use of the word. It is not a meaning we would ever have chosen. It applies to more circumstances than we would ever have dreamed. If you find glory here, you will find it everywhere—literally!

111

FOURTEEN

God and Government Glue

CONRAD A. SIMONSON

Then Moses and the people of Israel sang this song
to the Lord, saying,
  "I will sing to the Lord, for he has
    triumphed gloriously;
    the horse and his rider he has thrown into the sea.
  The Lord is my strength and my song,
    and he has become my salvation;
  this is my God, and I will praise him,
    my father's God, and I will exalt him.
  The Lord is a man of war;
    the Lord is his name.
  "Pharaoh's chariots and his host he cast into the sea;
    and his picked officers are sunk in the Red Sea.
  The floods cover them;
    they went down into the depths like a stone.
  Thy right hand, O Lord, glorious in power,
    thy right hand, O Lord, shatters the enemy.
  In the greatness of thy majesty thou overthrowest
    thy adversaries;
    thou sendest forth thy fury, it consumes them
    like stubble.

At the blast of thy nostrils the waters piled up,
  the floods stood up in a heap;
  the deeps congealed in the heart of the sea.
The enemy said, 'I will pursue, I will overtake,
  I will divide the spoil, my desire shall have its
  fill of them.
  I will draw my sword, my hand shall destroy them.'
Thou didst blow with thy wind, the sea covered them;
  they sank as lead in the mighty waters.
"Who is like thee, O Lord, among the gods?
  Who is like thee, majestic in holiness,
  terrible in glorious deeds, doing wonders?
Thou didst stretch out thy right hand,
  the earth swallowed them.
"Thou hast led in thy steadfast love the people whom
  thou hast redeemed,
  thou hast guided them by thy strength to thy holy
  abode.
The peoples have heard, they tremble;
  pangs have seized on the inhabitants of Philistia.
Now are the chiefs of Edom dismayed;
  the leaders of Moab, trembling seizes them;
  all the inhabitants of Canaan have melted away.
Terror and dread fall upon them;
  because of the greatness of thy arm, they are as still
  as a stone,
till thy people, O Lord, pass by,
  till the people pass by whom thou hast purchased.
Thou wilt bring them in, and plant them on thy own
  mountain,
  the place, O Lord, which thou hast made for thy
  abode,

> the sanctuary, O Lord, which thy hands have
> established.
> The Lord will reign for ever and ever."
>
> Exodus 15:1-18

MY FIRST TWO CHILDREN
(they are becoming so numerous that I find myself count-
ing them by two's) have a running argument about the
triune God, and how he acts in this world. One of them—
I think it is the four year old—has decided that God made
everything except the stars, and those are the particular
work of Jesus. Her brother and I regularly do our best to
get her to come and reason together with us. I have read
all the pertinent passages from Pieper, Aulén, Stump, and
the Book of Concord to her, none of which seem half so
convincing as her brother's threats to explain the gospel
truth by physical persuasion. But she, with the patience of
Job and the zeal of St. Paul, agrees with us, only to
announce her heresy again at the first sight of the glittering world of a star. Marcion was not half so durable.

My son has decided that I am God's helper, a fact that
he announces with far more persuasion than I am sometimes able to muster. At any rate, they find it quite likely
that God is doing things all around them. God is blamed
for every downpour and given credit for every flower. He
is regularly called to task for the chilling Canadian winds,
and as frequently encouraged to provide picnic weather.
They aren't old enough yet to recognize the amused and
patronizing smiles that their elders give them, so they go
on believing that God acts in such common fare as weather
and wind and even my own daily round of activities. It
will not be long now before they will know that most

grown-up people view their confident assertions with amused and sophisticated disbelief. Someday some kind-hearted soul will explain to them that rain comes from the interaction of the sun and the sea, and that stars either exploded or gathered into place.

Then they will have two possibilities before them. They may either discount God as an active agent altogether; or they may heartily and uneasily affirm that God used to do things, but that the Old Gentleman has been in early retirement for nearly twenty centuries, and now we wait for the great day when he will next take an active part in things. And whichever of the two they choose to believe, they will have come a long way from their present naive and Christian understanding of the world. They may very well be better theologians now than they will be when they have had the facts of life explained to them by some pious and irrelevant Sunday School teacher.

The Lesson for the Monday after Easter (Exodus 15:1-18) is a case in point. Most of us are reasonably ready to agree that God did great and mighty wonders when his people lived among the perfidious Egyptians. We recount the burning bush, the stick turned serpent, the plagues of fleas and frogs and the three day eclipse. To cap it off we detail the plague of death, and the piling up of the Red Sea into two walls which came tumbling down like a liquid anticipation of Jericho. The Lord, we solemnly tell each other, certainly used to engage in some sterling and startling demonstrations of his determination to have things his way.

We know that it is different now. God hasn't led anyone around with a pillar of fire or a moving cloud for ever so long. And how remote are the days when he last talked to anyone on a mountain! Occasionally a fit of common sense overwhelms us, and we harbor the gnawing doubt that God ever did work that way. Then it is that we wonder if the enthusiasm of the faith and glorified retrospect have not embellished what were remarkable but reasonable events. No sooner have we begun to wonder if the plagues of Egypt were not natural events, no sooner have we concluded that the crossing of the sea was made possible by the draining and drying effects of an opportune wind than we are dragged back to the impasse by our growing guilt.

Somehow it seems to be a denial of the hand of the Lord to suggest that these great events of olden times had comprehendable causes. The overbearing weight of our guilt feelings will let us say nothing less than that Moses' stick literally became a serpent, and back again; that the magicians of Pharoah had the same power; and that Moses was privileged to see God's backside only. No one who comes to our churches today expects God to accost him in a burning bush, or seriously expects the world to end this afternoon, or anticipates that his wife will be turned into a pillar of salt (however ardently and secretly he relishes that last prospect). It is only by developing a considerable lapse of common sense, or by virtue of self-delusion, that our contemporaries can accept the notion of the divine disruption of everything they rely on in this world.

Why do we ask it of them? We ask it of them because we have almost completely lost the sense of God acting within the framework of his own creation. We have so far removed God from participation in the stuff of this world that the only possibility we can allow is his outside interference. Even our children are better theologians than that. They will not concede, as we do, that God is a part-time deist. Somehow they will see him acting every day in the cause and effect, freedom and determination of this world. And they will see his will being done. They are so foolish as to think that I am his helper, whose time is spent inking a silk screen, whose diet is eternally flavored with government glue, whose advice to the troubled is spectacularly inept. They think that God acts in all the common things; and they are quite right.

Once two children of the Lord walked toward Emmaus, wondering about the events of the preceding week (cf. Luke 24:13-35). They were perplexed because they had thought that God might do great things in Israel, but Jesus had died like any other man. The kingdom had not come with a clap of thunder or even a revolution. And when a stranger came to walk with them, they asked him if he were the only man in Jerusalem who had not heard what had happened in the last few days. He in turn called them fools and reluctant believers because they were still not persuaded that God would act so ordinarily. He talked about himself, but they just couldn't see him.

When he took bread, and blessed, and broke it, and gave it to them—then he was known to them. In the breaking of bread. When one considers all the possibilities at his disposal, it is strange that our Lord did not call down a legion of angels, a little heavenly fire, or at the very least, show them the stigmata. But they knew him in the breaking of bread.

Sometimes I forget what it is like not to be a member of the household of faith. I spend nearly every day with holy things, forgetting that for many upon whom I call, I am their first reminder of the church in days, even weeks. I read accounts of other, more faithful men than I, hum the tunes and try to recall the words to hymns I have sung half a hundred times, and which they have never heard. Once one came to my Pastor's Class to learn something about the faith. He came only once. I think I know why. He listened to the others who were there. They were from Roman Catholic and Baptist and whatever churches, each trying to remember what he had been taught in his childhood. He had never been taught so he sat bewildered. We plunged into the scriptures with zeal and into a most imposing textbook with determination. When the evening was over, he never came back.

I had forgotten what the church looks like to someone outside her bounds. It wasn't that he simply didn't understand the vocabulary. He didn't understand our whole point of view. I think he would have understood Pharoah. We don't understand Pharoah very well. We sympathize with Pharoah's enemies who said that he was arrogant and blind and a liar, and who also wrote the scriptures. Pharoah was plagued with foul water and frogs and gnats and flies and boils and hail and locusts and death. Moses said that it was the Lord punishing him, and each time it seemed to Pharoah that it was so. He said to let the people go. But when each plague was over, he asked himself if he were out of his mind. He had seen flies and frogs and hail and death before—it wasn't necessary to blame the Lord. He sent his chariots after the people of Israel. The chariots could not go where the people had walked, and bogged down. The wind stopped, and the water came back again. Then Moses and the people sang: "I will sing to the Lord, for he has triumphed gloriously; the horse and his rider he has thrown into the sea" (Ex. 15:1). Pharoah cursed his rotten luck and a freak wind.

Sometimes when I kneel at the altar I feel that way. I wonder what idiocy it is that imagines this giving and taking of bread and wine to be the work of the Lord. Then I remember that it has always been that way. God doesn't come raging into the reason of this creation tearing great holes in the sense of things. God always acts like he does in the sacrament: in the ordinaries of life.

But, then, my children might have told me that.

FIFTEEN

The Eye of God

HERMAN G. STUEMPFLE, JR.

Now Sarai, Abram's wife, bare him no children: and she had an handmaid, an Egyptian, whose name was Hagar. And Sarai said unto Abram, Behold now, the Lord hath restrained me from bearing: I pray thee, go in unto my maid; it may be that I may obtain children by her. And Abram hearkened to the voice of Sarai. And Sarai Abram's wife took Hagar her maid the Egyptian, after Abram had dwelt ten years in the land of Canaan, and gave her to her husband Abram to be his wife. And he went in unto Hagar, and she conceived: and when she saw that she had conceived, her mistress was despised in her eyes. And Sarai said unto Abram, My wrong be upon thee: I have given my maid into thy bosom; and when she saw that she had conceived, I was despised in her eyes: the Lord judge between me and thee. But Abram said unto Sarai, Behold, thy maid is in thy hand; do to her as it pleaseth thee. And when Sarai dealt hardly with her, she fled from her face.

And the angel of the Lord found her by a fountain of water in the wilderness, by the fountain in the way to Shur. And he said, Hagar, Sarai's maid, whence camest thou? and whither wilt thou go? And she said, I flee from the face of my mistress Sarai. And the angel of the Lord said unto her, Return to thy mistress, and submit thyself under her hands. And the angel of the Lord said unto her, I will multiply thy seed exceedingly, that it shall not be numbered for multitude. And the angel of the Lord said unto her, Behold, thou art with child, and shalt bear a son, and shalt call his name Ishmael; because the Lord hath heard thy affliction. And he will be a wild man; his hand will be against every man, and every man's hand against him; and he shall dwell in the presence of all his brethren. And she called the name of the Lord that spake unto her, Thou God seest me: for she said, Have I also here looked after him that seeth me? Wherefore the well was called Beerlahairoi; behold, it is between Kadesh and Bered. And Hagar bare Abram a son: and Abram called his son's name, which Hagar bare, Ishmael. And Abram was fourscore and six years old, when Hagar bare Ishmael to Abram.

—Genesis 16:1-16 (AV)

"THOU GOD SEEST ME. . ."

These four words are inscribed on the wall above the pulpit in a historic church near my home town. You wonder why those who built the church chose exactly *these* words to stand before them when they came to worship. They are certainly appropriate enough, for the most profoundly true thing to be said about the hour of worship—indeed, about the whole of life—is not that we see God but that God sees us!

Yet those who built the church could easily have found more comforting words. It isn't always pleasant to be reminded that we're under the eye of God. Sometimes we wish we could escape his scrutiny. There are Sundays when

121

a text like this one would leap out from the wall like an accusing finger: "THOU GOD SEEST ME."

I

Significantly, these words were first spoken by a fugitive. Hagar was a runaway slave. And she had good reason to run. She had gotten herself involved in "the eternal triangle," using the child she had conceived by Abraham as a tool to dislodge her mistress, Sarai, from her place. Abraham, caught in the middle between two strong-willed women, took sides with Sarai and Hagar fled.

But in the wilderness she learned something. She learned that though she could escape her mistress, she couldn't escape God. The record speaks of an "angel of the Lord" who met her in the wilderness. Perhaps it was her conscience. It may have been a whisper of guilt that grew louder and more insistent each step she took. However it was, she knew God had caught up with her. Eyes she couldn't shake off were fastened on her back. So, at last, exhausted from her flight, she stopped in her tracks, turned around, and went back to face the snarl of evil she'd helped create. When it was all over, she could only say in hushed wonder, "Thou God seest me."

But this isn't only Hagar's story. It's your story and mine. We're all runaways of a kind, doing our best to outdistance our consciences when they accuse us, going out of our way to avoid a meeting with God when there's guilt on our hands. We bury ourselves in our work; we distract ourselves with amusements; sometimes we even throw ourselves into religious activities to cover up the sense of wrong inside. But there's no escaping the eye that follows us.

Sartre, in his play *No Exit*, pictures hell as a brightly lit room in which three people are condemned to sit through eternity with their eyes wide open. Each person sees the whole truth about the other two and the others see the whole truth about him. The lights never go out in the room and the eyelids of the three people never close. Each is sentenced to a full exposure of what he really is.

It's that way before God. Like a great sweeping radar, he detects the slightest motion of our wills and reads our thoughts the moment they form. He probes those obscure corners of our hearts in which we try to hide things from others, and even from ourselves. The disguises we wear in public mean nothing to him. Others may look upon us as successful, respectable, even religious, but he knows the truth about us. He sees us as we are. There's no place to hide from him. There comes what someone has called "the midnight hour when we must unmask" and acknowledge what he has known about us all along.

II

But if it isn't always a comfort to us that "God sees us," we should remember that it's no comfort to God either.

There are times when blindness—or at least the natural limitation of our vision—is a blessing. All of us who are parents are certainly better off for not being able to see every move our children make twenty-four hours a day, seven days a week. We catch our breath often enough as it is over the risks we see them take and the accidents they barely miss. Suppose our eyes could follow them every minute. The consumption of tranquilizers (already outselling all other drugs) would skyrocket. It's a good thing we don't see all and know all.

But God enjoys no such relief. His eyes are never shut. At least this is the way Scripture pictures him. ". . . he who keeps Israel will neither slumber nor sleep," a Psalmist tells us (121:4). He's testifying to the insomnia of God, his everlasting vigilance from which nothing is hid.

Think of some of the scenes he's watched: men killing and maiming each other on a thousand battlefields and dropping bombs on helpless cities; children starving on one side of the earth while wheat surpluses pile up like mountains on the other; people excluded from jobs and schools and houses because their skin is dark and then set upon with dogs in the street when they dare to lift their voices in protest. Everyone was upset recently when a debutante's "coming out" party went wild and wantonly wrecked a Southhampton mansion. Imagine how God feels about the way we have vandalized a world he created with infinite love and care!

God lifts the veil on his feelings in a scene in one of the Gospels. Jesus is riding toward Jerusalem at the head of a parade. People are waving palm branches and shouting that he is a king. Suddenly, at the crest of a hill, he sees the city spread out below him. This is the capital—the Washington of his people—the place for a ruler to lay hold of his power. But Jesus, the strong Son of God, bursts into tears. He weeps over the city. He weeps because beneath the glittering surface of pomp and piety he sees the malice and godlessness which will cause men to seize his life, God's gift to them, and crush it to pieces on a hill "outside the city wall." "Would that even today," he mourns, "you knew the things that make for peace! But now they are hid from your eyes. . ." (Luke 19:42).

But the tragedy of it all was not hid from *his* eyes, and

124

his eyes are God's eyes. In Christ we see God seeing us. The eyes of God in Christ aren't cold and appraising, like an auditor's going over the accounts—or like ours when we take the measure of somebody who's just tramped on us. His eyes are the eyes of a father who watches in anguish while we do foolish things from which he can't turn us without destroying our freedom. He looks at us through tears as we seize the gift of life and run off to far countries of rebellion, and he watches with compassion for us to come to ourselves and return home.

III

But God does more than watch. He follows us! Our lesson tells us that "the angel of the Lord found (Hagar) by a spring of water in the wilderness, the spring on the way to Shur." Shur was a place near the Egyptian border. It was about as far away as Hagar could go. But there in the remote wilderness she learned that God has pursued her. And somehow she sensed that it wasn't just because he wanted to settle accounts with her—to bring her back to "face the music" for what she had done in the household of Abraham. No—she sensed that God had followed her because he was concerned about her, even though she was nothing but a slave girl and in the wrong, besides. In spite of everything, God cared about her fate, and so he intercepted her in her flight.

It wasn't only or even mainly terror, then, that moved Hagar to cry, "Thou God seest me." It was grateful amazement. It was wonder and thankfulness that God, the Lord, the king of heaven and earth, did not overlook even so small and unworthy a creature as herself but followed her with love to this far place and to this low point.

In the end, then, it is our comfort that God sees us. *What* he sees brings anguish to his heart, and the *fact* that he sees strikes guilt and anxiety into ours; yet, in the end, the *knowledge* that he sees us is our only hope.

I think the ultimate despair in life is to feel that we are unseen. One of the characters in Thornton Wilder's play, *Our Town,* is a young woman who dies shortly after her marriage. In one of the scenes she is permitted to return from the dead for a day in her home. She moves among familiar things and familiar faces. *But nobody sees her.* And this isolation is more than she can bear. By the end of the day she longs to go back to her grave on the hill.

It's possible for us to reach such points in the midst of life—to feel that we move among people who never really see us in anything more than the most superficial way—to come to the conclusion that we've been tossed into some dark corner under a pile of troubles where not even God is aware of us. Perhaps there *is* no unseen but all-seeing one at the heart of the universe. What if it *is* just blind chance or the mindless, sightless monster fate that stands behind the mystery of life? Suppose there are no divine, eternal eyes that see us with clarity and compassion?

This, I think, is the way those Hebrew exiles in Babylon must have felt when they cried, "My way is hid from the Lord, and my right is disregarded by my God" (Isaiah 40:27). This was the sense of abandonment through which our Lord himself passed on the cross: "My God, my God, why hast thou forsaken me?" Yet, it is exactly because of the forsaken Christ that we know we are never forsaken. Because God came among us in our own human form to pass through the darkest, lowest points of our existence, we know that there is nowhere his eyes do not follow us.

Because we have seen God in Christ, we can say from our hearts, "Thou God seest *me*."

This pain, then, which you carry secretly about—the tangled mess into which you sometimes get your life—this loneliness into which no one else can enter—these responsibilities which seem about to crush you—all this he sees! You are not alone with it. You are known and loved in the midst of all the strains and stresses of your life and in spite of all your follies and frailties.

IV

"He who formed the eye, does he not see?" asks one of the Psalmists (94:9). "Yes, he does!" we answer. He sees all. Nothing is hidden from him, and there is nothing we can hide. But he sees it all with love and pity. Therefore, we do not cringe in terror under his gaze, but we lift our eyes with trust to his and acknowledge with thankfulness, "Thou God seest me."

The Hard,

Knotty Problems

of the Faith

SIXTEEN

A Perspective
on the Ascension

GILBERT E. DOAN, JR.

One Thursday each spring, unnoticed by most of us, the Christian world celebrates an important holiday. The ascension, which is said to have taken place forty days after the resurrection, is one of the several biblical events of major significance which are observed on weekdays. For Roman Catholics Ascension Day is a holy day of obligation. Not having holy days of obligation, and yet not wishing to lose sight of the ascension, Protestants have from time to time tried to move this festival to a Sunday. The Lutheran churches in this country have not tried to do this, but ever since Muhlenberg's time, the Sunday before Pentecost has been called "Exaudi: The Sunday after the Ascension." That kind of drags the ascension in by the heels, but at least it's an attempt to prevent its being altogether lost from view.

There's one small problem with this, however: the lessons for Exaudi, the Sunday after the Ascension, are already rustling with the promise of Pentecost, and the ascension seems to be forgotten. So we must go back to the Epistle for the Day of the Ascension of our Lord.

This basic lesson consists of the first eleven verses of the book of the Acts, which Luke begins by calling his readers' attention to "the former treatise," which is, of course, St. Luke's Gospel:

The former treatise have I made, O Theophilus, of all that Jesus began both to do and teach. Until the day in which he was taken up, after that he through the Holy Ghost had given commandments unto the apostles whom he had chosen. To whom also he shewed himself alive after his passion, by many infallible proofs, being seen of them forty days, and speaking of the things pertaining to the kingdom of God; And being assembled together with them, commanded them that they should not depart from Jerusalem, but wait for the promise of the Father, which, saith he, ye have heard of me: For John truly baptized with water; but ye shall be baptized with the Holy Ghost, not many days hence. When they therefore were come together, they asked of him, saying, Lord, wilt thou at this time restore again the kingdom to Israel? And he said unto them, It is not for you to know the times or the seasons, which the Father hath put in his own power. But ye shall receive power, after that the Holy Ghost is come upon you: and ye shall be witnesses unto me, both in Jerusalem, and in all Judaea, and in Samaria, and unto the uttermost part of the earth. And when he had spoken these things, while they beheld, he was taken up; and a cloud received him out of their sight. And while they looked stedfastly toward heaven, as he went up, behold, two men stood by them in white apparel; Which also said, Ye men of Galilee, why stand ye gazing up into heaven? This same Jesus,

*which is taken up from you into heaven, shall so come in
like manner as ye have seen him go into heaven.*
                                    —*Acts 1:1-11 (AV)*

THAT, BASICALLY, IS THE STORY.
But now this "ascension," this going up into heaven which
weekly we confess in the creed, presents, shall we say, a
few minor difficulties—matters involving the location of
heaven, the behavior of clouds, matters involving the law
of gravity, and whatnot. But these are difficulties which
are really not very much to the point. I get a little tired of
hearing about these insuperable barriers to intelligent faith.
This common disbelief in the ascension, which is blaringly
trumpeted abroad as the brazen atheism or the superior
skepticism of an enlightened scientific age, turns out on
inspection to be nothing more than a staunch unwillingness to admit that either science or theology has made any
progress at all in two thousand years. St. Luke, we gather,
is to be censured for knowing less than we do about gravity
or outer space. Why, you may as well chide the Sanhedrin
for never quite managing to get a man into orbit. St.
Luke believed, with everybody else including the best scientists of his day, that heaven was, geographically speaking,
"up" (where else?), and if, as it seems, this ascension affair took place on a cloudy day, then, of course, Jesus was
in the clouds. (Where else?) Of course the difficult thing
is that even today, two thousand years later, many people
still think of heaven as "up there," and therefore some of
these many, who really know better, doubly deserve the
reproof of the men in white; "why stand ye gazing *up* into
heaven?"

But there's something else you should realize. Appar-

132

ently, in all the earliest documents of the Christian community, there is no mention at all of the ascension. St. Paul himself, for instance, treats the resurrection and the ascension as though they were pretty much of a piece, and maybe took place on the same day. St. Matthew and St. John are completely silent on the matter, and St. Mark's and St. Luke's Gospels contain only passages on this matter which biblical scholars regard as of extremely doubtful authenticity. So as it turns out, this passage in Acts is probably only Luke's reporting of a tradition which began to develop only some years after the resurrection—at which time, of course, St. Luke had not yet come into the picture, and would not for several years.

All of which would presumably lead one to ask, why all the fuss about the ascension? Why is it even in the creed? Why does our church, having pretty much given the chance up of a real holiday on one Thursday each spring, nevertheless hang on to the ascension by the awkward expedient of lifting out the following Sunday? It might be better all 'round just to let it slip gracefully into oblivion—no?

Well, no. And I suppose the reasons for saying "no" fall into two categories. The first would be ordinary "common-sense" sorts of reasons, and the second category would be that of cosmic drama.

We can begin with the first. It would somehow seem necessary and fitting basically to end, somehow and sometime, the series of resurrection appearances which the risen Christ put in to assure his faithful ones that he had indeed conquered the last enemy, which is death. Again and again he had come to them, and the time soon approached when they were convinced that he was the victor, and when further appearances were unnecessary to their conviction. (And you might note here that it doesn't much matter whether this involves one day or forty. It's a matter of judgment.) The time did come to make an end and the ascension is the answer to the question of style. Jesus did something, which we call the ascension, to make it plain that he would be paying no more visits. Otherwise you can just imagine the confusion, what with people poking about looking for him and wondering what was wrong that he stopped coming around, and wondering where he had got to and what he was doing. (Look around you and you'll find folks doing *that* to this very day. . .)

And not only would they be wondering what had happened to him, but they would also be wondering what his resurrection meant for his relationship to the one whom he so often called his Father. Were the Father and his Son now alienated? Did one now have to make a choice between them? (Little did they know how complicated *that* matter was soon to get!) But was God the Father, now, to be blunt about it, in on all this? Did he approve? After two thousand years the answer seems so logical. It was not so obvious back then. St. Paul sensed this difficulty and felt he needed to write that Jesus did *not* count his equality with God a thing to be grabbed away from God, but rather, "being found in fashion as a man, he humbled himself, and became obedient unto death, even the death of the cross. *Wherefore* God also hath highly exalted him, and given him a name which is above every name: That at the name of Jesus every knee should bow . . . and that every tongue should confess that Jesus Christ is Lord, to the glory of God the Father" (Phil. 2:8-11 AV). In this sense, then, the ascension is the blessing, the seal of approval, of God the Father on the finished work of God the Son. Sitting at the right hand means, of course, among other things, being given the place of honor. And a place of honor is thenceforth reserved for the man who follows the way of the cross, who is not offended at being read out of the company of the righteous, and persecuted by those who think that they are thus doing God a favor.

These, then, are a couple of the common-sense reasons for the ascension; an obvious and meaningful end to the resurrection appearances, and the seal of God's approval on the life and work of this man named Jesus. There are many other reasons of this common-sense variety which make the ascension, or something very like it, a necessary episode in the narrative of Jesus' career.

But it seems to me that the second kind of reason is a more important kind. This is the kind of reason which sets this episode in the context not only of the life of Jesus, but also in the context of the whole sweeping drama of a cosmic redemption. You could outline that drama in five acts.

Act I begins with God, singular, solitary, and alone, brooding over the void. Then he sends forth his spirit and the universe and the earth are brought forth and flung into being in sheer creative exuberance. And part of this creation, by contrast ridiculous in number and proportions, is a peculiar wingless hairy biped called "man," whom, surprisingly enough, God creates "in his own image"—which, incidentally, means not that God is a wingless hairy biped, not that God has a mind and a memory and a language, or makes tools, but that man is made to be in communion with God. And God gives this little critter the top position in his creation—that is, a position of responsibility for managing the whole works as God's representative.

In Act II, this little creature gets altogether out of hand. He decides he is going to run this show for his own purposes, and that *he* is going to decide what's right and what's wrong—that is to say, he "eats of the tree of the knowledge of good and evil." He sets himself up as the Lord of creation and for that presumption is punished by God with death, with mortality, which is God's way of saying to him, "you have turned the earth rancid by your treating it as though you owned it. But no further. Be not deceived: God is not mocked. I am from everlasting to everlasting. From now on you have seventy years."

The next act is a long one, and sometimes tedious. It takes up most of the Bible. God now continues to put up with this little creature's whims, follies, and vanities, yet he keeps trying to reconcile the creatures to his own lordship. He chooses out one small race of them for his special attention hoping to work out through them the salvation of the rest of the world. Again and again he sends prophets to call them back to himself. Largely the prophets are ignored or stoned or sawed in half. He sets up a priesthood and the little creatures pervert it and corrupt it, turning it finally to their own glorification. And when this race called Israel goes too far, he raises up kings and armies in other countries and he uses them to punish his chosen people. Then his people repent and he raises up other armies to set them free again. Soon the people get fat and sassy again and have to be slapped down once more. Israel is a wayward child and learns slowly, if at all.

Things get hopelesser and hopelesser until, in Act IV (how Shakespearean!), in the fulness of time, God comes himself as a member of this race, this race now grown too dull and willful to see or hear him. He comes, the creator, to be a part of his own creation, to be one of those very men on whom the curse and punishment of death has fallen, to "be sin" for it, to bear its awful punishment . . . and then to rise victorious over death on behalf of all mankind.

For if by his descension, or incarnation to death, he did make himself one with the lost creation, so by his ascension did he bring the creation back to God's right hand, restored and reconciled at last to God. As St. Paul writes, "When he ascended up on high, he led captivity captive . . . (Now that he ascended, what is it but that he also descended into the lower parts of the earth [death]? He that descended is the same also that ascended up far above all heavens that he might fill all things)" (Eph. 4:8-9 AV).

And the fifth and final act is where you and I are living now. Across the world, by the work of the Holy Ghost, is a body of people called the church, joined both to Christ and to the world. And it is through them, by the power of the Holy Ghost, that Christ now works to complete the restoring of the whole world to the creator.

See, now, how essential the ascension is in the whole cosmic drama of redemption. If Jesus is only a divine emanation, gyrating supernaturally through a bit of space and time and evaporating again, then his ascension is nothing more than a pious frivolity and without any meaning for us or the rest of the world. But if in truth we are a part of his creation and also members of his body, then his work of reconciling the world to God reveals the importance of the ascension to him, to us, and to the world he came to save. Without it, the circuit is still open and nothing happens.

If this still seems a bit murky and abstract, think of it in terms of an analogy. This cosmic drama ends as a veritable open sea rescue operation. Picture a little outboard foundering in the swirling currents of a whirlpool. Picture the men aboard sick with exhaustion and the gas and the oars long gone. The boat is not yet lost down the funnel, but it veers closer and closer. A rescue cutter sights the boat, but cannot reach it or make fast to it for the sea is too rough and the men too weak to catch or hold a line. So the strongest man aboard the cutter takes a coiled line over his shoulder and dives into the waves. He swims to the little boat, makes one end of the line fast to a cleat, and swims the other end of the line back to the cutter, climbs aboard and makes it fast to a winch. There is still much to be done, to be sure, but in fact the boat has been saved.

Now, what good would it do for this heroic swimmer just to dive into the waves and get drowned? Or even join the men in the boat? Or even give them the rope? Or even bend one end to the cleat? Or even then jump out again and swim safely ashore? Enough said. He obviously has to get back to the cutter.

You will remember that before Jesus left his disciples he had a losing battle on his hands when he tried to convince them that it was expedient for him that he go away. They were to a man aghast at the prospect of his departure. But by and by, afterward, the expediency—slight understatement—came across clearly to them. And the account of the ascension in Luke's Gospel closes significantly, "They . . . returned to Jerusalem with great joy; and were continually in the temple, praising and blessing God" (24: 52-53 AV).

We can take our cue from them. For it was their salvation—and that of the whole world—that was at stake in the ascension. And your salvation and mine, too, for we are among the sick people in the outboard. And all the heroism of the man who plunged into the deadly sea for us avails us nothing unless he gets back to the cutter with the other end of the line. It was expedient for us, too, to put it mildly, that he go away.

SEVENTEEN

Your Shoes on Your Feet

GILBERT E. DOAN, JR.

ALL ACROSS THE COUNTRY and throughout the world, there are millions of men and women who, over the space of twenty or forty or sixty years, have knelt regularly before the altar at the Lord's Supper. For many of these millions it is hardly worth arguing that our Lord is "really present" "in, with, and under" the bread and the wine. For them all this is so true that while they cannot perhaps *explain* it, they are simply not inspired to launch out into passionate debate about it. They simply *know* it. Thus they believe and thus they teach.

But there are others for whom the "real presence," "in, with, and under" the bread and wine, is *not* so altogether obvious. I daresay there are some of these "others" here. There are the younger communicants among us who have not had the benefit of long and steady sacramental grace and fellowship. There are some recent converts to whom the clear and unquestioning belief of the old-timer or even of the ex-confirmand is a luxury far beyond their reach. There are the skeptics whose experiences with the church or with the world have led them to be pretty chary of taking people at their word in matters of vital importance, who have perhaps been stung more than once for being trustful.

And there are others, perhaps most of us, who from time to time just plain wonder what all these words mean really and whether what people *say* they mean is really true after all.

To these people, what happens in the Communion is simply *not* altogether plain. And there are but few who really give them any kind of satisfactory answers. "In, with, and under," they are told. And when they ask what *that* means, they are often simply told that it's all a mystery anyhow (which it is), and that we shouldn't *attempt* to *understand* it (which is not much help).

So, for many people the whole affair seems hopelessly vague and shrouded in mystery. And since no one really seems to know what this sacrament is all about, it's rather hard, you know, to understand why all these Lutherans have steered such a steady course away from intercommunion with each other, especially since they all say the same things about the meaning of the sacrament.

More than this, however, since no one seems to be able to explain just what happens in the Eucharist, you and I may ourselves be reluctant at times to be a part of something so unclear. If after several years of steady participation in the Lord's Supper there is no increase in the depth or richness or vitality of life, no clearer understanding of the loving will of God, no stimulus to the imaginative and authentic and faithful life, we may do well to call a halt, to stand aside for a bit, in order to see where the trouble may be.

What has gone awry? Is something wrong with this sacrament?

It is unlikely that anything is basically wrong with this observation as ordained by our Lord. Nor can you just dis-

141

miss with a wave of the hand the age-old testimony of the church to the grace and power of the sacrament. Best start with ourselves, realizing that what is wrong is most likely in us—our attitudes, our understanding, or even so simple a thing as a lack of preparation.

But if we can assume that we are not holding against someone a grudge of the kind that can frustrate the forgiveness of the sacrament, and if we can assume a real hope and desire for a fresh start and a new direction in our lives, and if we can assume that we ask in prayer to be enlightened and helped to understand and fully participate in the Eucharist—if we can assume all this and *still* we run into a blank wall, then perhaps it becomes pretty clear that what is missing is a bit of plain effort to *find out* what Communion means. And a few hours' honest thinking and reading are worth many months of respectable and dutiful attendance at the altar in the wistful hope that somehow the fog will blow away all by itself. No one can do that thinking for us. *Least* of all can the preacher be expected to understand so well that no one else has to!

And when you think it over for yourself, let me suggest one technique. If the threadbare cliches and shibboleths cut no ice, if it doesn't help to repeat ten times "in, with, and under," or "not just spiritually but really present," then forget the old mottoes. Start somewhere else. There are literally dozens of ways of approaching the matter. Let me suggest just one of them—*Passover*.

In St. Matthew's account of the supper (Matt. 26:17-29), the word Passover appears three times in the first three verses. That's not insignificant. So let's think of the sacrament in connection with the Passover which is celebrated every year in millions of homes across the land.

What does the Passover say about the Holy Communion?

First: it says *expectancy*. Turn back to Exodus now and get the flavor of the Passover. Stand with the men of ancient captive Israel and hear *their* "Words of Institution." And as you listen, notice that there is a looking forward in the Passover institution and not just a memory. "When the Lord shall bring thee into the land of the Canaanities . . . which he swore unto thy fathers to give thee, a land flowing with milk and honey . . . (then) thou shalt keep this service in this month" (Exodus 13:5, AV). "When the Lord shall bring thee into a land flowing with milk and honey!" The Passover pointed to a glorious consummation for the children of Israel. One of the Passover prayers reflects the expectation of the kingdom soon when Passover will be celebrated in Jerusalem by every Jew. A phrase from that prayer is, "next year in Jerusalem." And at a dramatic moment in the ordinary household ceremony the door of the house is flung open to receive Elijah who is to come bearing the news that the messiah approaches.

And our Lord gave to *his* Passover the same forward look: "For I say unto you, I will not any more eat thereof, until it be fulfilled in the kingdom of God" (Luke 22:16). Remember those typical words of our Lord to the twelve: "Ye are they which have continued with me in my temptations. And I appoint unto you a kingdom, as my Father hath appointed unto me; That ye may eat and drink at my table in my kingdom, and sit on thrones . . ." (Luke 22:28-30). How glorious the consummation at which our Lord was hinting here! There was something to look forward to!

The Passover which Jesus celebrated with the twelve was a ceremony already steeped in anticipation, in tiptoe expectancy! So how come we Christians keep looking back to

143

Holy Thursday, refusing to participate in the looking forward which was the keynote of the Last Supper itself?

So how come we Christians, who believe that the Messiah has arrived, remember only the details and the tragedy of the passion? The lightning of the kingdom has flashed from the open tomb. He is risen! And we now live in the split-second of eternity between that lightning from the open tomb and the final thunder of the kingdom. Lift up your hearts! Lift up your heads! And the King of glory shall come in!

First, then, expectation. And *joy*. The Passover was a time of joyful expectation of the fullness of joy. Now listen. Remember the Easter sentence? "Christ our Passover is sacrificed for us." "Christ our Passover." But it doesn't end there. It ends with a *Hallelujah!* As the Easter hymn has it, this is "the Passover of gladness." "Christ our Passover is sacrificed for us. *Hallelujah!*"

So how come? On the face of it, a passion, a crucifixion, is a pretty peculiar affair about which to be shouting hallelujahs. No so! Not so even for ancient Israel. For them the blood of the Passover lamb meant freedom. It meant immunity from the fatal plague that was about to strike the families of their Egyptian slavedrivers. It meant freedom from decades of grinding oppression and servitude. It meant the promised land flowing with milk and honey—precious scarce commodities among the Jewish slaves in Egypt. And the blood of the lamb was smeared on the doorways of those about to be liberated, and then they ate the lamb.

What to them was the death of the lamb? Not something to be morbid about. It was the foretaste of the milk and honey of the promised land. It was the symbol of

God's mighty act for their redemption. So the blood of our Passover lamb was shed for our redemption—and we partake as did the twelve. And it is the occasion for joy: he is our deliverance from all that keeps us oppressed at heart and in bondage to ourselves and to the living death that walks our streets behind the masks of life. Why should we ruminate now on our own past bondage to sin and death from which he has come to set us free? Take and eat! Take and drink! The blood of Christ, shed for thee!

For sheer enthusiasm about eating and drinking the New Testament has no parallel. Again and again in the New Testament, the kingdom of heaven is compared to a great feast, a messianic banquet, symbolic of the joy of the host of the people of God redeemed by him from the fogs and anxieties and cares of the world. The Communion is the foretaste of the Messianic Banquet. Can we really be mournful? Lift up your hearts! Let us give thanks unto the Lord!

Expectancy, then, and joy. And now a third.

You know, when we think of the Communion, we think of it pretty much as a private affair and we ask ourselves, each of us, "what really do *I get* out of all this?" Can we square this with the Passover, which is what Jesus understood the Last Supper to be?

From Exodus again: "Draw out and take you a lamb according to your *families*" (12:21, AV) . . . it wasn't an isolated, private affair, but a *family* affair. "And it shall come to pass when your children shall say unto you, What mean ye by this service? That ye shall say . . . . by strength of hand the Lord brought us out from Egypt, from the house of bondage" (12:26-27; 13:14, A.V.). It was not only a family affair, it was a *family celebration*—a celebra-

tion of the mighty acts of God victorious. Ever try celebrating something big all by your lonesome? "For Passover," writes Rabbi Bernstein, "families gather from near
and far. Even the prodigal, the cynic, the skeptic returns.
The atmosphere is festive; the service includes ancient gay
songs and games for the children."[1] There is gladness remembering the new birth of a nation under God, a victorious God, knitting together a people as he redeems them
from desperate slavery. A modern Jewish poet has caught a
hint of the celebration and the holy joy:

> Prosaic miles of streets stretch all around
> Astir with restless, hurried life, and spanned
> By arches that with thunderous trains resound,
> And throbbing wires that galvanize the land:
> Gin palaces in tawdry splendor stand;
> The newsboys shriek of mangled bodies found,
> The last burlesque is playing in the Strand,
> In modern prose all poetry seems drowned.
>
> Yet in ten thousand homes this starry night,
> An ancient People celebrates its birth
> To freedom, with reverential mirth,
> With customs quaint, and many a hoary rite,
> Waiting until, its tarnished glory bright,
> Its God shall be the God of all the earth! [2]

Do you begin to see why we speak of *celebrating* the
Eucharist, and as a family, rather than just receiving the
elements as individuals? The Eucharist is the *celebration*
of the act of God in cross and broken sepulchre by which,

[1] Philip S. Bernstein. *What The Jews Believe.* (New York: Farrar,
Straus, & Young. 1950.) Page 61.
[2] Israel Zangwill. *Children Of The Ghetto.* (New York: Jewish
Publication Society of America. 1936.) Quoted by permission.

with a strong arm, he redeemed us from ourselves and from the demonic powers of the world and knit us together into a family, the family of Christ. This is the Lord's doing, and it is marvelous in our eyes! Celebrate with the rest of the family! "Therefore with angels and archangels and all the company of Heaven," the company of earth praises and magnifies him forever!

Let me now suggest one more echo from Exodus. Part of the chapter instituting the Passover reads as follows: "And thus shall ye eat it; with your loins girded, your shoes on your feet, and your staff in your hand; and ye shall eat it in haste: it is the Lord's Passover" (12:11, AV). The children of Israel, you remember, were about to set out on the long and perilous safari through a trackless wasteland. This was the mission on which they were being sent as a part of the plan of God. It would soon come to seem endless. Many would die on the way. They would rebel and long even to be slaves again, if only they could get back to their homes in Egypt. But now they had to be ready to set out at a moment's notice: "Thus shall ye eat it, with your shoes on your feet."

And thus shall ye eat the Lord's Supper, with your shoes on your feet, and ready with an obedient will to do the bidding of God.

There is a time, to be sure, to take off your shoes, so to speak, as the Lord commanded Moses: "put off thy shoes from off thy feet, for the place whereon thou standest is holy ground" (Exodus 3:5, A.V.). Yet men are prone to carry it too far. They seem inclined to pad about the holy places in stocking feet for the rest of their lives. So it was at the Transfiguration of our Lord. Peter and James and John would have preferred to stay there basking in the

147

glory of the Lord, building little sanctuaries, as they said, "one for thee, one for Moses, and one for Elijah" (Matthew 17:1-8). But the old adage has the truth of it: "the true atheist is the man whose hands are cauterized by holy things." So it was that instead of lingering to soak up the atmosphere of the mountaintop experience, the three men suddenly found themselves down on the plain again, and surrounded by a throng of invalids and lepers, all begging to be healed.

As surely as the three men had been allowed to stay on the mountaintop, their experience would have degenerated into the atheism of ceremonial. As surely as the ancient Hebrews had stuck around to enjoy the Passover festivities, they would still be in Egypt. And as surely as you and I concentrate on the atmosphere and the sanctity of the Communion, forgetting the hard journey on which we are sent, we shall fail to understand even vaguely what the Communion is about.

For the Communion is the sacrament of our freedom— and of our journey—the journey from each day into the next, each day with its bewildering maze of bank statements, inscrutable textbooks, disturbing letters, soured relationships, chaotic headlines, and formless anxieties. You and I do wish from time to time for the blissful ignorance of childhood or for a life of happy paganism, as the Israelites hankered after the fleshpots of Egypt. But ever again, along the way, stands the Eucharist, the thankful celebration of our release from childish self-centeredness, the constant nourishment along the way of mature and powerful living. And if you're not ready to do the living, if you come with your shoes off, you'll miss the whole point of it.

Has it seemed to you for some months that at the altar

you've somehow been missing the gift and the point of it all? Remember the Passover. You come not just recalling the past and not just to get a personal gift. Rather you come looking forward, on tiptoe, to the God-shaped, joyous destiny of his people. You come as one small part of the countless family of God to praise him for his mighty act of deliverance from the powers of darkness. And you come with a willing and ready obedience and girded up for the next day's mission on which he sends you. "Thus shall ye eat it, with your loins girded and your shoes on your feet."

EIGHTEEN

Faith: A Posture of Living

MORRIS J. NIEDENTHAL

*For while we live we are always being given up to death
for Jesus' sake, so that the life of Jesus may be manifested
in our mortal flesh.*

—*2 Corinthians 4:11*

ROBERT PENN WARREN IN HIS NOVEL
The Cave tells of an old man facing a painful death by
cancer. Recalling the vitality of his younger days and con-
trasting it with his approaching death, the old man says,
"I reckon that living is just learning how to die and dying
is just learning how to live."[1] Contrast his posture of living
with that of the fellow who says, "Living is keeping from
dying and dying is the end of life." The two postures are
exactly opposite, aren't they? Both could hardly be true.
Maybe neither is.

Yet I dare say that most people assume one posture or
the other. Conceivably they are torn between the two—but
they cannot have it both ways at the same time.

The apostle Paul's experience confirmed that of the old
man. He said, "For while we live we are always being
given up to death for Jesus sake." His words suggest that

[1] *The Cave.* (New York: The New American Library. 1960.) p. 381.

death isn't simply a biological fact, the heart's final surrender. Nor is it simply the fact with which the mortician
deals when he closes the casket, lowers it into the grave,
and shovels dirt on top. Paul's words may well include this
last episode in each of our life stories, but they point
beyond it to something even more general. If he can say
that we are *always* being given up to death, he must be
referring to something in our common, everyday lives.

Perhaps he is using the word to point to our experience
of never being able to stand still but always being carried
on to the next moment, the next day, the next year. We may
smash our clocks to pieces, yet our time keeps ticking away.
We can't stop it. We can't make it last. Nor, on the other
hand, can we dispose of it without disposing of ourselves.
Death, then, is the experience of being thrown into the
river of time which flows as irreversibly forward as the
Mississippi flows from its origin in Minnesota to the gulf
of Mexico. Each ripple of life endures for an instant and
then flows on. We always experience the end, the death of
a moment—and in each moment is the reminder of our
own end, our own death, our own being no more. There is,
as we all know, no going back up stream.

Have you ever gone to a family or class reunion? Many
of them are terribly sad affairs, or better, melancholy affairs. Past episodes are recalled and shared. Gaiety and
laughter may prevail. Yet, beneath it all one can also sense
a certain melancholy. Things *have* changed. Those remem-
bered days *are* past and gone. We can never quite get
around it. I've often wondered whether this isn't the reason
why so many reunions end up as drunken brawls. Times
have changed. The "rah-rah" days are gone. Let's drown

our melancholy and pretend. Then we will be, as A. E. Housman put it, "sterling lads" again.[2]

Poets in all generations have lamented the slipperiness of time, its elusive and passing nature. Listen again to Housman:

> Into my heart an air that kills
> From yon far country blows:
> What are those blue remembered hills,
> What spires, what farms are those?
>
> This is the land of lost content
> I see it shining plain,
> The happy highways where I went
> And cannot come again.[3]

Do you sense his melancholy, his experience of death, of passingness, of the end—"the happy highways where I went / and cannot come again"?

But the poets are not alone. Have you ever wondered why we often cry during moments of intense happiness and joy? You know what I mean. A towering basketball player comes forward to receive a trophy for his team's victory and breaks down in tears. Why the tears? They are so out of place. Could it be that they are triggered by the sub-concious awareness that this moment of happiness will not last, it will pass on, it too will die?

We are always being given up to death, to the passing and dying moment. No sooner are we born than we are on our way to death. An infant's first struggling breath for

[2] "Terrance, This is Stupid Stuff."

[3] From "A Shropshire Lad"—Authorised Edition—from *The Collected Poems of A. E. Housman.* Copyright 1939, 1940, © 1959 by Holt, Rinehart and Winston, Inc. Reprinted by permission of Holt, Rinehart and Winston, Inc.

life is taken under the sentence of death. Someone put it wryly: "None of us will get out of life alive." The cards are stacked against us.

The pressure of death's power on us is constant. Every anxious moment, every unavoidable crisis, every fear, every love involves the presence of death. They show death's power and presence. Consider several examples—we don't have to hunt for them. A young mother is terrified when she hears her infant son gasping and struggling for breath in his bout with the croup. Why the terror? Is it not because she knows the precariousness of life, the possibility of the child's dying? Or again, why are we so anxious and often defensive, so quick to defend ourselves against criticism or accusation? Is it not due to the fear of being nobody? But to fear being nobody, wanting to be somebody— this fear is really the fear of death, isn't it? What is death but being nobody?

Consider also what it means to love. The venture of love always involves the risk of death. A lover pours out his heart and life for his beloved. One day she is critically injured in an automobile accident and dies the following morning. In her death, the lover also dies a bit. He is left alone with no one to share the private and secret memories they had together. That's the way it is with death. He is the "great closer of doors" but only after he has robbed two or more lives. Rarely does he take only one at a time. But, you see, had the lover not cared, had he not loved, he would not have had to risk death and his experience of being alone. Loving always involves risking death.

The experience of death—in the sense of inevitable passing on, of being nobody, of our final end—is the commonest experience we have. The old man dying of cancer may have been right—"Living is just learning how to die and dying is just learning how to live." This much is certain: the other fellow who claimed that "living is keeping from dying and dying is the end of life" was spawning a lie. Death is the commonest experience you and I have.

Note again that the apostle Paul affirms as much. He knows that we are always being given up to death. But this isn't entirely a senseless waste for him. Listen again. "We are always being given up to death for Jesus' sake: so that the life of Jesus may be manifested in our mortal flesh." How odd, how strange that the life of Jesus should be manifested in the arena of death. We might have chosen a more pleasant and cheery place for his life. Thank God, *he* didn't. Thank God he manifests his life in the midst of death. If he hadn't, there would be no word of the Lord for my life. If God has a word for my life, then he will have to speak it in the face of death. I have no other life than the one in which the power of death is constantly present. None of us has. That Jesus shows forth his life in the midst of death means that God is present for you and me in the commonest experience of our everyday life.

Moreover, he shows himself to be our God in conquering and overcoming our experiences of death. This is what faith is. Faith is a posture of living in which God proves himself to be God in overcoming death. It is learning how to die. It is the confidence that my life with all that threatens it ends not in death but in God. The apostle Paul said, "I am sure that . . . (*nothing*) can separate us from the love of Christ" (Romans 8:38-39). Nothing can separate us because everything ends finally not in death, but in God.

Our experience of the constant flow of time ends not in an ocean of nothingness, but in God. The hymn writer said

—"Time, like an ever-rolling stream bears all its sons away; They fly forgotten, as a dream dies at the opening day." This is not faith's talk. It is a nightmare. A credible one. But it isn't faith. Faith dares to hold that time bears us home. Faith is not a flying "forgotten, as a dream dies at the opening day." It is a steady trek through the night to the dawn of homecoming. To march through life both knowing the terror of night and being open to God's every coming to us to still the restlessness of the night—this is faith.

Our anxious moments, which show death's power, do not end in death but in God. A man suffering an incurable disease was spending an anxious and restless night. He couldn't sleep. At last he recalled several hymns he had learned as a boy. These reminded him of Psalm verses he had learned in confirmation class. Finally, his restlessness was conquered and he went to sleep. His anxious moments did not end in death, but in God. And he slept. God proved himself to be his God in conquering his fear—this is faith.

Our fear of being nobodies ends not in death but in God. A salesman I know is moved around the country from place to place as effortlessly as a checker is moved on a board from one square to another. He complains of being a nobody, only an economic unit of power. Unfortunately, his experience is not an exception in these days of complex structures of power—government, corporations, unions, associations. Beneficial as these may have been, they have, nevertheless, often crushed a person with the ease of a steam roller flattening a mouse. The threat of being nobody is real. Yet to hear in the presence of it a voice that says, "I know you. For I am he who was despised and rejected by men, he who was treated as a nobody, pushed out of the city, marched up a hill and hung on a cross to die. That's where they put me. But in rejecting me, they pushed me toward you and made it possible for me to bear with and carry your rejection. For in the rejection of me, the rejection of you was included. In my name is your name and the name of all nobodies whom my Father considers somebodies and whom he will in no way forsake." To hear that word in the very moment in which we are treated as nobodies, to cling to it—this is faith.

Luther expressed all this so well in one short and unforgettable sentence. "Faith," Luther said, "is the darkness in which Christ lives." Mind you, he did not say that faith transforms darkness into sunshine. No. The darkness remains darkness. Tomorrow may well confront us again with the mute, dull and monotonous flow of time. Tomorrow the sick man will probably endure restlessness again. Tomorrow the salesman will probably be reminded that he is still nobody. The darkness remains. The power of death is still felt. Yet, to discern in that darkness Christ present and living for me, holding and keeping my life—this is faith. Paul expressed it this way, "We are afflicted in every way, but not crushed; perplexed, but not driven to despair; persecuted, but not forsaken; struck down, but not destroyed; always carrying in the body the death of Jesus, so that the life of Jesus may also be manifested in our bodies" (2 Cor. 4:8-10). Faith includes darkness, it knows we are being given up to experiences of death. But it also knows Christ living in that darkness. Faith is the experience and confession of *"but not;"* but not crushed, but not forsaken, but not destroyed.

The old man said, "I reckon living is just learning how to die, and dying is just learning how to live." Faith doesn't simply reckon: it dares such a posture. Faith risks dying in the sense of letting one's life go. It risks death in the sense of loving and caring as the mother cared for her child, and the lover loved his beloved. It risks the anxious moments of being nobody. It risks spending one's life in the present moment instead of trying to hoard and keep time from passing. Faith risks this not because any of us is able to bear these experiences by himself. Faith dares them, dares to give itself up because it knows God proves the sufficiency of his care in our weakness.

Dilsey, one of the remarkable characters in the fiction of William Faulkner, shows this daring and courageous quality of faith. Being a large spirited and compassionate house-maid, Dilsey spends and wastes herself by forever picking up the responsibilities which members of the Compson family drop. She shoulders the burdens of raising the Compson children despite the insults Mrs. Compson and the children heap upon her.

Dilsey is free to bear with and suffer for others because, as she puts it, "I've seed de first en de last . . . de beginnin en de enden."[4] And she saw both in a single person, Jesus Christ, who breaks the tyranny of the past by his forgiveness, and the terror of the future by his promise of hope. And in this freedom, Dilsey receives the courage to be truly present for those near her who are in need—this is faith.

At the end of Luther's Order for Morning Prayer, he

The Sound and The Fury. (New York: Modern Library. 1946.) p. 313.

157

appended this sentence: "And then shouldst thou go with joy to thy work." Such is the simplicity of faith. It is the confidence that our days and nights are in God's hands. It is a posture of living created by him who lives, speaks, and reigns in the midst of death. And because he reigns there, he can be your God and mine.

NINETEEN

He Called Her by Name

JEROME W. NILSSEN

Easter

Jesus said to her, "Woman, why are you weeping? Whom do you seek?" Supposing him to be the gardener, she said to him, "Sir, if you have carried him away, tell me where you have laid him, and I will take him away." Jesus said to her, "Mary." She turned and said to him in Hebrew, "Rabboni!" (which means Teacher).

—John 20:15-16

SHE THOUGHT HE WAS THE GARDENER. It was dawn, when day and night are locked together, and she could not quite see through the gray air. Then, too, she was weeping, sunk in a watery vision of agony and death. The name and the face . . . Jesus, Jesus, Jesus . . . must have been in the rhythm of her being: she must have called that name and seen that face a thousand times since the last time, when he was dying. She could have called that name a million times—and what good would it have done? She saw him die.

In a sense, one death is all deaths. And every death is

Death itself. To see a person die is to look into a magic mirror and see the last death of all—one's own. I have seen several people die; not many, perhaps, but enough. There seems to be enough waste and purposelessness in this business of dying to make a man sick for centuries. I can remember calling the names of some, calling, first questioningly, then like a witless fool, desperately—as if I could stem the tide.

There was a moment with one, a very brief moment, when I think I would have given my life to have hers spared. But what good would that have done? What could I have saved her from, what could I have gained for my-self? The fact is, I did no more than call a name, sound a word, stir the air, reach toward the unreachable. And that meant nothing at all.

And when it was over, there was a dark wave of nausea, a sense of helpless suspension over a hungry sea. And now, when certain names and faces drift back to me, part of me that is dead rouses and stirs uneasily, a regretful ghost that gives no peace. But I could do nothing then, I can do nothing now. What is the use, if death is the end? And when I think on death, I have only bad dreams and a gloomy prospect.

For hours I thought that it had all been a mistake. I thought, after I had seen the thing happen, that someone would come along to rectify it all. I thought that if I could only retrace my steps, return to that room, return to that time when I called her name, she would rise up and answer with my name. Perhaps I had used the wrong inflection or the wrong tone the first time. I thought, if only I could try once more. It is not enough, you know, to talk about pleasant memories, good days shared under better circumstances. Because the old black man is a ruthless one; he doesn't leave anything behind; he isn't satisfied with anything less than the whole person, and he's happier yet if he can take something of you along with him. But the name; yes, the name, he left that behind, and he wouldn't care if I did retrace and return to pronounce it again in a hundred accents. He had the flesh and blood that filled it. If I had her name, still he had smothered the voice that could speak mine. And that made all the difference in the world.

It made all the difference in the world because it closed off part of my world: death is the great closer of doors. They shut one after another until you find yourself in a bare room and the door behind you shuts too. And time, that was once viewed as possibility, becomes the engulfing horror of nothing, nothing at all.

So death makes time stink of decay and rottenness. But here is the worst thing about the old black man: he turns love into darkness. In love one person lives as much as is humanly possible in and for another: in love one person becomes two and two become one. Then death enters and has his mocking way; and when he condemns the beloved he holds a trial for the lover, and he says, "All right, keep loving, and you will shine your life into pitch blackness, and the blackness will come after you and swallow you up. Or else deny your love, keep your life to yourself and pretend that such a thing as love never existed." And the lover can call the name of his beloved, and call and call; and nothing, nothing at all, will come back to him: he will give and give and give, and nothing at all will be returned to him—until finally he will give himself up to the darkness.

Or else he will simply deny love. And that way too the black man gains his peculiar happiness.

People nod and admit, "Death must have his day." But they give insufficient credit to death's ambition. Death wants not merely one day out of a person's life; he wants every day; he wants a denial of every moment of breath and bone and blood, a denial of the flesh and taste and touch of love. He wants darkness, now and forevermore.

And Mary moved in darkness near the tomb. And she heard someone (she thought it was the gardener) say to her, "Why are you weeping?"

If it had been the gardener, he very well might have asked the same question, "Why are you weeping?"—not denying, accepting that people have a reason to weep, but wondering why, what door was closed for this woman that she should be filled with sorrow. If it had been the gardener, Mary might have answered, "Because he is dead, and now I don't know what to do with myself." Then the gardener, if it had been the gardener, might have shrugged his shoulders and gone about his business: people live and people die, the grass keeps growing; the graves settle; the flowers wilt; but like the grass, the gardener's work survives. He likes it best in the morning. He has a cool place, and quiet; and he is the last man at the end of the world. He keeps busy and suppresses his imagination: some days he enjoys the company of the gravedigger, though they speak very little to one another, and only in the most general terms. Somehow they feel they are trespassers and ought not to speak at all: yet deep down, beneath the province of language, they are grimly aware that this *is* home.

And here is Mary, going to stare into the darkness of the tomb, weeping for what might have been. Here is Mary, in a shaded world a shadow meeting another shadow, whom she supposed to be the gardener, a tender of deathbeds.

But he isn't the gardener. He is one who comes out of the darkest of darknesses and knows her name and speaks it, "Mary." This is not merely a voice or a spirit or a word mysteriously scrawled on a rock. This is a person, a living person reaching out and speaking to another person, saying, "Mary."

And standing in the very eye of that upheavaled and violently still, hurricaned morning, Mary has the faith and the courage and the presence of grace to answer, "Rabboni!" Here is all the love and life she had sent hopelessly into the depths now returned—to her, personally. Here is nothing less than the complete victory and vindication of love in Jesus' naming of the woman and her response.

He, Jesus, had been dead. There was no doubt about *that*. A hundred pounds of spices had been stuffed into the black tomb with his dead body, and now that tomb, unplugged and open to the air, was redolent of the sickening-sweet, too-obviously disguised smell of death. He, Jesus, had been carried dead into the black, hungry maw that is the destiny of all men. Every hammer blow on the cross had been the sound of another door closing; and then the last door was rolled into place, and Jesus' time was closed and his life was cancelled out.

Jesus came to an end behind that last door. There is no mistaking that. But the door opened again—I do not know how, God knows. But the door did open; the same door that death had shut, God opened. And so God made the end into a new beginning.

And Mary? The love she had given to him he took into the tomb; and then he emerged and returned it to her, whole and complete. For Mary the resurrection was not so much a rising-up as it was a returning, a returning and a new beginning—an exclamation that nothing has been lost, everything has been discovered. The once-dead, un-bright cinder of a world was sparked again, and her name was the flint that struck the fire. She was cold, and her name on his lips set fire to the world; her name on his lips was sun and moon and stars, it was the world made all over again for her. The sun was high in the sky, and she could find her way out of the graveyard.

Of course, to follow Christ means to die with Christ. Mary knew this. This is why she stood weeping in the dawn, weeping not only because something of her had died with him. She had been present at the end, and part of herself had suffocated in the closed tomb. But now, with this return, she was free to make a new beginning.

Perhaps this is the hardest thing to understand about this event we call the resurrection; not that Christ came back from the dead, but that he came back as a person speaking to other persons, calling them by name, giving them back the life and the love they thought they had lost forever in the grip of death. In this restoration there is a new freedom. And it is difficult to analyze, difficult to describe precisely.

All I know is that when the old black man comes to try me and to mock me, saying, "All right, keep loving, and give your life up to the darkness," I have an answer for him. I can have a turn to mock him, saying, "All right, I will," because whatever love I surrender in the name of Christ to the threat of darkness will burst through the darkness and live on.

Pride does not prompt me to say this, nor toughness of character. I think that even if Christ himself were to put his hand into mine I would still be afraid of death. But to be afraid of dying is another matter. For dying is the antithesis of living, the denial of life, while death is the hard last act of life. The dying man fearfully accepts death's sentence long before the last act, and he fearfully acknowledges the futility of love and the steady draining-away of life into nothingness. He hears the doors closing, and he weeps to himself, softly and hopelessly.

The dying man, however, is more than countered by the man who lives in following Christ. I mean the man who, like Mary, walks with Christ even to the cross, and there gathers the vision that his cross is all crosses, his cross the prefiguring of the last stance of the whole race. Thus there is none but one crucifixion, and his last breath a moaning of and for and by every child of man. And upon this breath the man who walks with Christ drifts down, emptied, to the tomb.

But this is not the end of the story, for there is yet restoration to the fullness of life in the returning Christ who hands back faith and courage and evokes the tremulous responses of giving and loving. He brings back to life those who, like Mary, have believed that caring for the dead is their only choice. He uncovers freedom, the freedom to live into the heart of death, giving and giving, giving love and life to the most hopeless tasks; the freedom to accept death as an end, and at the same time, the freedom to act in the faith that there is no end that does not disclose a new beginning. In leaving the tomb and confronting Mary, Christ has shown a new way, not a way out of life, but a way into the heart of life. This is the way into death, but then through death into freedom.

This is the hard way; to say Yes to death, to sink into time and death again and again, giving freely to death precisely that which he wants most, life itself; so to be utterly emptied—and then to say, *Yes, there is light, there is an opening that Christ has made,* there is a restoration that Christ is able to give, even though restoration seems impossible. This is the hard way; to give so completely of life and love that nothing is left. All doors seem shut, all hope of retracing one's steps is lost—and then, in faith and courage, to respond to Christ and follow him out of the graveyard, to live again. This is the seizing of possibility where there is no possibility, the affirming of life where there is no life, the breathing of fresh air after all the doors have been shut, the accepting of freedom when time has ticked off the last second: this is a sensing of all that Jesus meant and did when he compressed all names into one and spoke a word of recognition, "Mary."

Yes, it is a miracle that Jesus burst through death and returned without reservation to life. But it is equally miraculous that Mary had the faith and the courage to take up this impossible freedom that was handed to her in the sound of her name, "Mary." It is miraculous that in the midst of death she dared to stop dying, she dared to take up her freedom to mock death, she dared to respond, to live and to speak, saying, "Rabboni!"

But this she did. God knows how, to him the praise.

TWENTY

Jesus Was No Angel

LEE E. SNOOK

St. Michael and All Angels

"See that you do not despise one of these little ones; for I tell you that in heaven their angels always behold the face of my Father who is in heaven."

—Matthew 18:10

LET ME TELL YOU THAT I HAVE been in a state of acute consternation all week. I had been warned several weeks ago that today would be the day of St. Michael and All Angels, a day which rarely falls on a Sunday. This, I knew, would also be the Sunday that many new students would worship with us for the first time. It might be proper, I thought, to say some things about fulfilling one's responsibility or vocation as a Christian student in the modern world. But it was certain that the whole liturgy today would be dominated by lessons full of horses and chariots of fire, of angels watching over little children like god-fairies, of Michael and his angels battling against the dragon and the dragon's angels. Clearly, these lessons could not be allowed simply to dangle in the service with no comment or examination.

Frankly I was irritated that the church could be so anti-quarian and superstitious as to allow St. Michael and All Angels to remain in the liturgical calendar. And there were certain of the faithful in the congregations who had also let it be known that they were gleefully curious just what the preacher of the day would choose for a text! With this bit of background I hold up to you my chagrin: how does one preach about angels to a sophisticated university congregation?

By the time I had finished researching and sketching the broad outlines of my sermon, however, I concluded that the church in all her wisdom was not antiquarian and superstitious for preserving this blessed and holy day in the liturgical calendar. Rather, the holy church actually protects all of us from false doctrine and pernicious belief! Really! But, you see, I still don't believe that angels put the stars out at night and I won't believe that or anything else about angels until I can see them. Even then, I would probably keep quiet about it unless other people were see-ing them too!

The preacher's task, then, is the same this morning as at any other time: namely, to inquire what it can possibly mean for us today that Jesus said at another time and an-other place: "See that you do not despise one of these little ones; for I tell you that in heaven their angels always behold the face of my Father who is in heaven."

I

If we are at all interested in what the Bible says, we have to be interested in angels. To put it another way, not to be interested in angels is not to be interested in the Bible. We can't say: "Don't bother me with all that mythology, just give me the heart of the Bible's point of view; tell me what it actually means." The Bible's point of view or message includes more angel-stories than we have time to mention. Angels and angelic beings cannot be ripped out of the Bible in any way which would preserve its proclamation. In other words, we are stuck with angels even though we may never see one or be one.

Angels are ubiquitous in the Bible and appear at the most crucial times. It was an angel who told Abraham in the nick of time, "Hold it, you don't have to sacrifice your boy." Another angel was on hand to tell Moses what was really going on when that bush caught fire and wasn't burned up. It was an angel who made all the smoke which shielded the escaping Hebrews from the pursuing Egyptian armies (the world's first protective smoke screen). Of course, these angels—who look like handsome, even beautiful men, who probably know everything—are found in other ancient literature besides the Bible. The biblical writers, in fact, got some of their ideas about angels from the Akkadians, Hittites and Egyptians. The Hebrews were not the only people who had special divine helpers in such dangerous times as war. Read the Iliad and you will discover something similar.

In one sense angels are commuters who travel regularly between heaven and earth (remember the story of Jacob's dream?). The notion of commuting angels was popular in other parts of the ancient world. In Egypt the graves of the dead were often equipped with long ladders so that the deceased could more easily climb out of there and on to heaven. And in Genesis 6 there is a hint of something going on that is more explicit in Greek literature: angels, or beings called sons of God, start to consort with human women until God put a stop to what was unfair competition with mortal males. And there are other kinds of angelic beings: cherubim and seraphim for example. A cherub was not a little cupid with a bow and arrow, looking like a sweet little fat-faced choir boy, but rather a being with a human head, the body of a large animal and at least one pair of wings! In 2 Samuel there is a reference to God touring the heavens seated on a cherub, presumably making an inspection trip of the universe (22:11).

When the Hebrews were forced to live among the Babylonians, they improved their knowledge of angels considerably! In Daniel and in the apochryphal literature, references abound more and more. Angels are charged with the operation of all natural phenomena in the heavens and in the earth. How does God get all his work done? The angels, of course! They even set up a kind of union or hierarchy—or like chickens, they have a pecking order. The top-most angels are, of course, the archangels, then there are regular angels and below them the angels of presence and the angels of sanctification. In some places there are references to military angels, like a celestial Salvation Army. There are friendly angels (like those under Michael) and there are hostile angels. Some of them are specialists. Some seem to be in charge of obstetrics and do nothing but announce that a baby is on the way. Others, long before Freud, used dreams to issue warnings and to probe for deeper meanings beneath the surface of events. Others, like criminal lawyers, just got people out of jail, as with St. Peter in the Acts. Each nation had a patron angel, like a heavenly ambassador to a United Nations in the sky. Finally, there are other heavenly beings who simply stand around the throne of God and do nothing but make joyful noises in praise of the Lord.

Now we would miss the point entirely if our only reaction were to ask, "Must I, as a Christian, believe all of that?" Rather, we have to see this whole scheme of angels and heavenly beings for what it was: namely an ancient cosmology, a fanciful way of explaining how everything worked. To put it another way, it was part of a rather unscientific science like phrenology, astrology or alchemy.

II

It was into such a world that Jesus was born. It was widely accepted that the way things happened up in the skies, or among the living things of the earth, or within the societies of men could best be explained by the presence of angels and other "elemental spirits," as St. Paul called them (Gal. 4; Col. 2). It is not too far from actual fact to say that this whole system was a kind of natural science, or a principle of explanation regarding the natural world. Admittedly, this was the popular view, the view of the masses. Long before Jesus was born there had been some shrewd observations made about such things as the curvature of the earth and the like; but that sort of inductive science was rare. Except for the aristocratic Sadducees, nearly all of the contemporaries of Jesus merely assumed that angels, powers, principalities and elemental spirits were operating all the time and in everything.

We can assume, then, that Jesus believed in angels. The particular class of angels of which he speaks are "the angels of presence" which we refer to as "guardian angels." Jesus could speak as innocently of angels as he could speak about birds which are personally fed by God or of the lilies of the field which receive God's special care

171

and attention. What are we to make of this naïve attitude in the man, Jesus of Nazareth? Are we to conclude that we have to reject such a teacher as our model because, after all, Jesus is irrelevant to our world-view? Or ought we to conclude that because Jesus is unlike any other man who ever lived, we had better believe that he knows more about the way things work than anyone else? Jesus believed in angels. Must we therefore either dismiss Jesus as irrelevant or believe in them because he did?

The fact that Jesus believed in angels should not surprise us, but should merely confirm for us that he was a very secular man. Jesus was a secular man to the extent that he did believe in angels and thus accepted the world view of his own age. That is what makes him secular, the fact that he was very much a man of his own age, his *saeculum*, his own generation. He had absolutely nothing new or startling to say about the operation and function of the world. So secular was he that people said of him, "Is not this Jesus the son of Joseph, whose father and mother we know?" His contemporaries knew him as one of them, knew him as another Jewish kid who grew up with them. Because Jesus belonged to his own age and accepted his own *saeculum,* he never thought to contradict it. He never said, "You know, it actually is not one of God's angels who pushes the lily up out of the ground and makes it grow."

So Jesus was, then, a secular man. He was a man of his own age and world precisely because he accepted its world view—even with angels announcing births and feeding birds. But remember what he also said in the Gospel for today, "Woe to the world for temptations to sin!" (Matt. 18:7). What do we make of that warning? A key incident in his life gives us the clue.

172

Jesus had just been baptized into his ministry and was spending a period of solitude and meditation in the wilderness. And he was tempted. One of his temptations was to jump off the tower of the temple and let God's angels rescue him (as Psalm 91 says they would). Certainly that would have attracted some attention and a following. But he would not do it. He refused to be seduced by the world view which almost all the people uncritically accepted.

Therefore, although Jesus was a secular man, a man who accepted the world view of his time, he did not absolutize that world view. Even the angels are not to be regarded as absolute or final or eternal or ultimate. Jesus could accept his own age and at the same time exercise independent judgment over it. His own age did not seduce him: it did not distract him from his calling, his vocation, his obedience to God alone. For him the circumstances of the age were not an excuse to tempt God.

III

The church indeed has been wise in preserving the day of St. Michael and All Angels because we are thus reminded that our Lord was a man of his age, a secular man who accepted the world view which prevailed during his lifetime. At the same time that we are perhaps astonished at the secularity of our Lord, we are also confronted with his independence and freedom. How could he stand in judgment of that very age which he accepted? He believed in angels, for example, in the same way that we believe in the law of gravity or the principles of chemistry and biology, but he wasn't seduced by the beauty, complexity and wonder of that world view so that he could be distracted from his mission. He could say, "Woe to the world

—which includes angels—or to any world for temptations to sin."

We are now at a point to understand our text, "See that you do not despise one of these little ones; for I tell you that in heaven their angels always behold the face of my Father who is in heaven." Here Jesus is using the total imagery of his own age, a heaven above in which whole galaxies of angels tend the stars and the creatures; and at the same time he is saying: "You take care that nothing ever becomes so important to your life—no career, no established way of life, no political ideology, no precious economic sentiments, no personal holdings or securities, no research proposal—that you try to justify in the name of that desire any exploitation or harm to those who cannot help themselves." Nothing is more important in this world than that all men, regardless of how deprived or helpless they may be, be assured a future.

As Christians, then, we are called not to believe all that Jesus merely accepted as part of life, but to be as Jesus was: secular—that is persons of our own age and generation. At the same time we are to be as Christ to our neighbor. And that means that in the very structures of our *saeculum* our lives are to take the form of the cross because it is in the cross of Christ that we see the reality and the truth of human life. It is there in the cross that we see what it means to be a man. To be a man as Christ our Lord was a man is to exist for others; it means that we are called by that cross to know the same obedience that Christ knew. To obey God is to believe that nothing in this life is so important that it can ever justify harming the little ones, the helpless and disenfranchised of the world.

For you who are students, what does it mean to take

the form of the cross in your life? Does it mean quitting
school and running off to the slums or elsewhere where
people are now helpless? No . . . not yet, at least. You
must first become secular, know your own age. Learn
about the world, about hygiene and biochemistry and bac-
teriology and economics and political power structures and
agronomy and what lights up men's aesthetic senses. But
then you are going to be tempted. Possessing knowledge
will be for you like Jesus knowing about the angels who
would save him. It will be power in your hands. Now,
with this power will you trample down all the ignorant,
the incompetent, the illiterate, the dispossessed of the
world because you imagine that you as university grad-
uates deserve the best for yourselves?

"See that you do not despise one of these little ones"—
for it will be despising Christ himself.

An American poet writing in the *Atlantic Monthly* recently discussed the nature of "facts." He says "doubtless
in that inter-stellar junkyard (which man) is beginning to
create he will learn new facts and these will lead him to
the knowledge of other facts. But no fact man ever learns
will tell him who he is, or why he is here, or what life,
or love, or death or beauty means."[1] The man of Nazareth
who lived in an age when angels were regarded as facts
also died—and to know what that death means is to know
who you are and what your life means. To know the meaning of that death is to know that Jesus is the Christ who
calls us to our true humanity as creatures of God.

[1]"Fact and Fancy" by Edward Weismiller. *The Atlantic Monthly.*
Vol. 212 No. 4, October, 1963 p. 94.

TWENTY ONE

The Vision of Pentecost

LEE E. SNOOK

IN MANY WAYS, THE DAY OF PENTECOST is a source of embarrassment to a majority of the Christian churches. On this day we remember that the Holy Spirit descended on an early gathering of Christian believers and baptized them with such power that they were able to do marvelous things. But after Pentecost, and for the rest of the church year, we generally ignore the Holy Spirit, allowing the so-called Pentecostal churches—those which we called the "holy rollers" when I was an irreverent youngster—to capitalize on their conviction that the Holy Spirit will move and excite those who submit themselves to the right kind of praying, singing and foot-stomping. Consequently, on the fringe of the whole Christian community are many enthusiastic, sectarian churches which are convinced that we staid, well-ordered Lutherans, Presbyterians and Episcopalians are not true believers because we are not moved by the Holy Spirit.

We ought to be embarrassed about this criticism because there is enough truth in it to hurt. We are rather reserved and dignified in our religious life. There is not much observable evidence that the Spirit of God has warmed our spirits. Of course, if we should consciously try to warm ourselves up a bit with the Holy Spirit, would it then be

the Spirit which makes us enthusiastic or some psycholog-
ical mood of good will and joviality similar to that of a
Rotary luncheon? When we start talking about the Holy
Spirit in such a critical, analytical way, as I am now doing,
we are sure to deflect much of the Spirit's work by our
very talk. It seems to me that if we are going to let the
Spirit of God be the Holy Spirit, then we ought not feel
that we can manipulate him by techniques, or that we can
get some intellectual grasp on him, reducing him thereby
to an abstraction of the mind.

I propose: first, to review the event of Pentecost as it
is written in the Acts; second, to offer this event as a fleeting, momentary vision of what a perfect community of
Christians would be like; and finally, to observe that Pentecost is still important and relevant to the present life of
the whole church.

I

Let's begin by recalling the whole event called Pentecost. You know, of course, that this story appears in the
second volume of the writings of Luke. His first book,
the Gospel, is one of four accounts which detail for us the
life, teachings, death and resurrection of Jesus. The second
book, the Acts of the Apostles, is the only one of its kind
in the New Testament, and it is in this book that Luke
undertakes to continue the story of those faithful ones who
were left behind after the resurrection and ascension of
Jesus.

You remember that during his lifetime Jesus had promised his disciples that they would not be left alone after
his death, but that God would send the Comforter who
would lead them into all truth. So far as we can gather

from Luke's story, the original apostles—now reduced to eleven after the suicide of Judas—did very little to carry on the work of Jesus except to choose another to take the place of the betrayer. As witnesses to the resurrection they had a great story to tell, and yet did little more than keep their group together, with Peter acting as the chief spokesman. Then came the day of Pentecost, a Jewish holiday, and all the believers gathered in one place. The absence of Jesus was painful to them and yet they could no longer expect him to appear among them because according to Luke, they had already seen him ascend to the Father in heaven. There were about one hundred twenty in the gathered assembly and with them were a number of devout Jews from all over the Mediterranean area. It was then, apparently without warning, that it happened.

The way Luke describes it, there was some sort of heavenly sound, and it looked as though tongues of fire came to rest on all those who were gathered, prompting everyone to speak in different languages and dialects which could be understood by the many foreigners who were there. Certainly what Luke intends to convey is that the people were moved in a wonderful way by the Spirit of God. They became aware of a mighty presence which made it possible for them to be drawn together in a wonderful harmony. In temperament, nationality, language, culture, and social class, each person there was different from the others, but the presence of the Spirit was manifested in such a way that they were transformed into a harmonious fellowship. They did not become a homogeneous, classless or undifferentiated collection of people; they were in fact even more aware of their differences. But whatever the visitation of the Spirit was like, what it did was to create

178

out of this diverse gathering a harmonious fellowship without destroying individual differences.

For purposes of our present understanding of what took place, this is what seems the most startling feature of the whole episode: those who were visited by the Holy Spirit were *freed to be themselves* in all their individuality and yet were drawn into a *harmonious fellowship* with the others, and together they proclaimed the mighty works of God. Perfect freedom and perfect harmony were derived from the Spirit's visitation. Aren't these the characteristics imagined for every ideal social order; individual freedom and social harmony?

However, the sequel to Pentecost is told by Luke with total candor. It isn't long until the church fails to sustain its balance of freedom and harmony. Not only do Annanias and Sapphira disrupt the community, even Peter and Paul have a basic dispute about policy. Still later, Paul has a sharp contention with Barnabas. It was also Paul, the missionary saint, who got bitterly involved in a conflict with the church at Corinth, directing to it his most stinging rebuke: even when he apologized, he did so with something less than complete graciousness. The perfect freedom and complete harmony which the church had fleetingly experienced on Pentecost evaporated as soon as the community set about to do its work.

II

What does it mean that the primitive church could not continue in the elevated and ideal circumstance of that first Pentecost when both perfect freedom and complete order prevailed? It was a real experience, to be sure, but an experience which was basically a *vision* of that which is

179

beyond the realm of simple possibility in human life.

Permit me to respond to that question in terms of my own life—which is probably not so different from yours. Before we were married my wife and I shared a kind of dream, a vision let's say, that in our home two conditions would always be present: first, the freedom of each person to be himself or herself—marriage would not be an enforced conformity; and second, the family would always be harmonious and well-ordered. It was a nice dream. But I now know that it will always be just that, a dream and never a reality. It is simply beyond the realm of possibility to allow even one member of the family to have perfect freedom and then imagine that we could preserve family harmony for that one person inevitably abuses his freedom at the expense of a well-ordered household. When one tries to bring about order and harmony, it is immediately apparent that not even the slightest degree of peace is possible unless every member of the establishment is coerced into giving up some of his freedom. That is, order is established not by the Spirit but by force. Well, I still have that dream of a family in which both freedom and harmony exist, but it is only a vision, a naive, innocent vision which can never be fulfilled.

Pentecost was a powerful experience which impressed on those first Christians the reality of the true community of believers, a reality in which each person is free to be himself, but is also able, by the power of God's Spirit, to live in harmony and good order with every other free individual. Even so, we learn from the New Testament itself that this was not the state of things in the day to day life of the early church. The church quickly learned, and has learned again and again through the centuries, that the

doctrine of original sin is powerfully true. There is a per-
sistent tendency in all men to abuse their freedom. By ig-
noring their own personal limitations, men exaggerate
their own rights to freedom and this exaggeration is always
at the expense of someone else's freedom. The events of
every age reinforce this conviction; to have personal freedom simultaneously with social harmony is not a simple
possibility.

Visions, or visionary experiences such as that of Pentecost, have led to some grave extremes. We could even say
that visions are risky because they can lead to fanaticism.
Whenever we believe that a vision can be easily translated
into the actual, real experiences of human life, it always
leads to a dangerous excess. One such excess is that of the
Pentecostal groups we have already mentioned; I mean the
extreme of believing that an absolute religious freedom for
the individual within the church is a simple possibility.
Individuals then tend to try to outdo each other in having
the most bizarre and extraordinary kind of conversion, or
in speaking in tongues in the most elaborate way. St. Paul
deplored such excesses because they were divisive to the
church. The other excess is that of supposing that within
the church a complete harmony of all believers is possible
or even required. We sometimes see this extreme among
Lutherans who insist that the only true unity is uniform
loyalty to "pure" formulations of doctrine.

To put it quite plainly, the experience of Pentecost cannot be duplicated in human life because Pentecost was a
fleeting, momentary experience which cannot be translated
into concrete historical actuality. But the Holy Spirit continues to work in the church by creating in us a desire, a

hope for that fellowship in which there is both freedom to be oneself and harmonious good order.

III

Although the perfect fellowship of believers in which both freedom and harmony exist is an impossibility within human history, Pentecost nevertheless has relevance for the church in every age.

First of all, Pentecost is relevant if we permit its vision to be a judgment on the present day church, including this congregation. After all, we can hardly be self-satisfied when we observe all too painfully that in our church a person is often not free to be himself but is almost pressured into pretending to be something that he is not. And we can hardly be self-satisfied when we observe the all-too-frequent examples of disharmony and the lack of good order in our fellowship. Pentecost provides us with a perspective from which we can judge ourselves and our church. I consider that judgment to be close to a divine judgment because its standard is God's Spirit-visitation on Pentecost. Perhaps we can allow this one observation from a human point of view: the extremes of fanaticism which are rooted in the notion that Pentecost is a simple historical possibility—whether that fanaticism is disorderly Pentecostalism or spiritless preoccupation with church busyness —often lack the ability to be self-critical precisely because their adherents suppose that they *already* have actualized the experience of Pentecost. Only when we allow Pentecost to remain a *hope* can it also be a perspective, a standing-place from which we can view our present church critically. When it becomes a simple possibility for history, we lose our ability for divinely inspired self-criticism.

Secondly, Pentecost still matters not only because it is a perspective for self-criticism, but also because it is for us, a source of hope and salvation. It is a vision of that for which we hope. When we think of heaven we ought to think not of countless identical heavenly beings, but of perfect freedom and perfect harmony between unique and different persons. Any vision which we might have of such freedom and harmony is a hopeful and saving vision, not just because it takes us beyond the here and now, but because it helps us in the here and now to work for greater degrees of personal liberty as well as social order. It is only because I have an ideal for family life that I am able to make the daily decisions and adjustments which can at all make family life approach that ideal. It is only because we have fleeting visions of what the fellowship of the church ought to be that we can make the day by day decisions and week by week adjustments to bring about approximations of that perfect fellowship which we can only have in heaven. The vision of Pentecost is a saving vision because it guides and controls as it judges and directs the life of the church in this world.

Pentecost is a vision which is relevant and which matters to the church today because it judges the church and also offers hope and guidance for the church in the present world. But Pentecost also reminds us that the Holy Spirit still visits the church—not according to some technique of worship and not because some churchly organization can guarantee it—but whenever the people of God have been caught up by an awareness of the awful *holiness* of God or even the distance of God. When we are taken up by the sense of the terrible other-ness of God, or let's say the sense that he is far beyond us and beyond our control, then we have been visited by the Holy Spirit. To know the Holy Spirit is to know that God is totally beyond our control and that our first action is to be still and know that God is God.

If you have ever read Franz Kafka's brief novel called *The Trial,* you will remember the anguish of the hero who has only the initial 'K' as a name. He is called before a strange court, accused, tried and sentenced. His sentence is never to know of what he was accused and convicted. You soon guess that this is the plight of all men. We go through our days in the ambiguous, unclear and unsettled state of never knowing perfection—but also in a state of never being too sure just what it is of which we are guilty.

We are informed by the gospel that we can never make ourselves perfect, but that through occasional and fleeting visitations of the Holy Spirit, we can catch Pentecostal visions of what perfection is. Perfection is impossible for us; we cannot live in both freedom and harmony. We can only learn to trust that God is willing to accept us and to declare us righteous out of his own pure love and mercy and forgiveness.

TWENTY TWO

The Shape of Hope

JOHN W. VANNORSDALL

NOTE: This is the final of three meditations given at a church convention. The first was on *The Shape of Joy;* the second on *The Shape of Freedom.*

THE SHAPE OF JOY IS to be conformed to the humble Servant.

The Shape of Freedom is the bondage of Christ to the will of God.

The Shape of Hope is the experience of failure.

This is one of the most profound insights of the gospel; that the shape of hope is the experience of failure.

"Pastor, how can I really know my God." "Run my son, run hard. Run to the scriptures, search their pages, Genesis to Revelation.

"Pray, my son, pray hard, pray often, pray when you wake and when you go to bed, pray when you walk and pray when you run.

"Do right, my son, do right at all times and in all places, do right by old ladies and in the parked car under the plane tree,[1] do right in all the earthy places."

"And shall I succeed?"

[1] cf. Archibald MacLeish, *J.B.* (New York: Houghton Mifflin, Sentry Edition. 1961.) p. 23.

"No, my son, you shall fail."

"Shirra in six orbits will seem more real than the Garden of Eden, and the trivial promise of tomorrow more relevant than the breaking of the Seventh Seal. Prayer will flow for a time and dry. Old ladies will stand in the buses, and young women under the plane tree will ask to go home. No, my son, you shall fail, and until you do, there is no hope, so run, my son, run hard to fail."

You will understand this:

That it's when we've tried our best to be like God and failed, that we are open to the one who comes to proclaim that he alone is God.

It's when we've tried to be good and righteous and failed, that we are open to the Christ who bestows the gift of righteousness.

It's when we've blasted the heavens with our prayers and fall dry and empty that the Holy Spirit fills our lives with the assurance of his presence.

Tell me what you have done, and I will rejoice with you. Tell me your failures, and I will show you the shape of hope sprung from the failure of the grave.

> You know failure in preaching, but God brings forth saints born of his grace.
>
> You know failure as parent, but God brings forth from your offspring men and women of integrity and piety.
>
> You know failure in benevolences, but out of the pittance God brings forth seeds borne recklessly on the winds of the Spirit which take root in strange places and in wondrous ways.
>
> Out of the failure of the grave, God brought forth a new people.

Out of the failure of the monastery, God brought forth
a reformation of his Church.

And we also shall run and fail, and out of this failure,
God will show us the shape of hope.

"Brethren, I do not consider that I have made (Christ)
my own; but one thing I do, forgetting what lies behind,
and straining forward to what lies ahead, I press on toward
the goal for the prize of the upward call of God in Christ
Jesus. Let those of us who are mature be thus minded . . ."
(Phil. 3:13-14).

NOTES ON THE CONTRIBUTORS

H. GEORGE ANDERSON
  Professor of Church History, Lutheran Theological
  Southern Seminary, Columbia, South Carolina

PAUL F. BOSCH
  Lutheran Campus Pastor, Syracuse University
  Syracuse, New York

GILBERT E. DOAN, JR.
  Northeastern Regional Director, National Lutheran
  Campus Ministry, Philadelphia, Pennsylvania

RICHARD QUENTIN ELVEE
  Chaplain, Gustavus Adolphus College
  St. Peter, Minnesota

PAUL J. HOH
  Pastor in the Lutheran Church in America, and
  Member of the House of Representatives, Common-
  wealth of Pennsylvania from Reading, Pennsylvania

ROBERT W. JENSON
  Department of Philosophy, Luther College
  Decorah, Iowa

WILLIAM H. LAZARETH
  Dean and Professor of Systematic Theology,
  The Lutheran Theological Seminary at Philadelphia,
  Pennsylvania

RICHARD LUECKE
  Director of Studies, Urban Training Center for Christian Mission, Chicago, Illinois

MARTIN E. MARTY
  Associate Professor of Church History at the Divinity
  School of the University of Chicago and Associate Edi-
  tor, *The Christian Century*, Chicago, Illinois

Morris J. Niedenthal
Assistant Professor of Functional Theology, Lutheran School of Theology, Maywood, Illinois

Jerome W. Nilssen
The Board of Parish Education of the Lutheran Church in America, Philadelphia, Pennsylvania

Conrad A. Simonson
Doctoral Student in Christian Theology, The University of Chicago, Chicago, Illinois

Lee E. Snook
Pastor, The Lutheran Church of Ithaca and Lutheran Chaplain at Cornell University, Ithaca, New York

Herman G. Stuempfle, Jr.
Professor of Homiletics, Lutheran Theological Seminary Gettysburg, Pennsylvania

John W. Vannorsdall
Chaplain, Gettysburg College
Gettysburg, Pennsylvania

Andrew J. White, III
Doctoral Student in Community Organization and Politics at Western Reserve University
Cleveland, Ohio

THE PREACHER'S PAPERBACK LIBRARY

Volumes already published:

1. *The Servant of the Word* by H. H. Farmer. 1964.
2. *The Care of the Earth and Other University Sermons* by Joseph Sittler. 1964.
3. *The Preaching of F. W. Robertson* edited by Gilbert E. Doan, Jr. 1964.
4. *A Brief History of Preaching* by Yngve Brilioth. 1965.
5. *The Living Word* by Gustaf Wingren. 1965.
6. *On Prayer* by Gerhard Ebeling. 1966.
7. *Renewal in the Pulpit—Sermons by Younger Preachers* edited by Edmund A. Steimle. 1966.

Further volumes are in preparation.

Type, 11 on 13 Garamond
Display, Garamond
Paper, Standard 'R' Antique